The History of Special Education

THE HISTORY OF
SPECIAL EDUCATION

A Struggle for Equality in American Public Schools

Robert L. Osgood

Growing Up: History of Children and Youth
Priscilla Ferguson Clement, Series Editor

Westport, Connecticut
London

Library of Congress Cataloging-in-Publication Data

Osgood, Robert L.
 The history of special education : a struggle for equality in American public schools /
Robert L. Osgood.
  p. cm.—(Growing up: history of children and youth, ISSN 1938-6095)
 Includes bibliographical references and index.
 ISBN 978-0-275-98913-2 (alk. paper)
  1. Special education—United States—History. 2. Children with disabilities—Education—
United States—History. 3. Educational equalization—United States—History. I. Title.
LC3981.O83 2008
371.90973–dc22   2007028377

British Library Cataloguing in Publication Data is available.

Library of Congress Catalog Card Number: 2007028377
ISBN-13: 978–0–275–98913–2
ISSN: 1938–6095

First published in 2008

Praeger Publishers, 88 Post Road West, Westport, CT 06881
An imprint of Greenwood Publishing Group, Inc.
www.praeger.com

Printed in the United States of America

The paper used in this book complies with the
Permanent Paper Standard issued by the National
Information Standards Organization (Z39.48–1984).

10 9 8 7 6 5 4 3 2 1

Contents

Series Foreword

The history of children and youth is a relatively new field of study that has been growing especially rapidly since the 1970s. Before that time, although there certainly were some historians who studied young people, they were few in number. Historians studying a particular topic or time period sometimes touched upon the history of children and youth in passing, but rarely were youngsters alone the subject of serious historical research.

However, in the last thirty years of the twentieth century and continuing to the present, children themselves have increasingly been objects of interest to historians. The experiences of young people in schools (both public and religious), institutions (such as orphanages and juvenile reformatories), and voluntary organizations (such as the Boy Scouts) have been the subjects of study. So have the toys children play with, the objects they live with, and the ways youngsters spend their money. Historians have also examined how young people have influenced the larger culture through their dress, their music, their dances, the movies and TV they watch, and the political action they take—especially during the Civil Rights Movement. Children living in certain time periods, such as the Great Depression, and children growing up in different parts of the country, such as on the western frontier, have been subjects of serious study. Many aspects of the lives of boys and girls, such as their encounters with the law, with the medical establishment, or with family loss, abuse, poverty, disability, work, war, discrimination, and class, have also been examined.

The purpose of this series, *Growing Up: The History of Children and Youth*, is to introduce this growing field in history to a larger audience. Authors of books in the series both synthesize much exciting work in the history of young people and present additional original research in the field. Books in the series emphasize the history of boys and girls, as well as children of diverse ethnic and racial backgrounds, and children from various social classes. Each book also covers a substantial period of time, and, as much as possible, their authors showcase the experiences of children themselves rather than exclusively adult perspectives on the young.

This book by Robert Osgood is a comprehensive evaluation of how disabled children have been treated in schools and institutions in the United States since the nineteenth century. Serious historical research on disability, like serious historical research on children, is relatively new, and Osgood puts the two together to provide a comprehensive overview of an important subject. He begins by examining how urbanization, industrialization, immigration, and the growth of the Progressive Movement affected children and altered attitudes toward disability in the late nineteenth and early twentieth centuries. He demonstrates how local and state governments began to provide special education programs in public schools first in urban areas, and much later in rural ones. He also examines how residential institutions for disabled children grew, especially those for the mentally disabled, the deaf, and the blind. By the mid–twentieth century, programs that isolated disabled children either in institutions or in special classes and sections of public schools were typical throughout the country. Osgood shows how such isolation affected disabled children and how public views on separation of the disabled from the general student population began to change by the 1960s and 1970s. Inclusion and mainstreaming became the watchwords of this later era, and remain, to this day, the most accepted ways of dealing with disabled youngsters.

For this study, Osgood inevitably relies heavily on records of public schools and public institutions. He turns a critical eye on these records and on the observations of teachers of disabled children to present a portrait of the experiences of such youngsters in the nineteenth and twentieth centuries. Not until the mid–twentieth century are there many testimonies from the parents of disabled children or from the children themselves. The limited historical record means that Osgood is not able fully to realize some of the goals of the series. He does not isolate the experience of disabled children by race, ethnicity, or even much by gender. He does assess the experiences of disabled children from different parts of the country and from different social classes. Osgood's study provides an excellent introduction to the important developments in the history of how disabled children in general have been treated since the mid–nineteenth century, and how they and their parents have reacted to that treatment, especially in the last half century. He ends with a provocative evaluation of how the education of disabled children has changed over time and what may be the patterns of such education in the future.

On a personal note, I would like to conclude by remembering that this book series began as one jointly edited by myself and Jacqueline Reinier, a fine historian of eighteenth- and nineteenth-century children and a dear friend and colleague. Jackie died of cancer before this series came to fruition, but without her support, it never would have begun. Thanks, Jackie!

Priscilla Ferguson Clement
Spring, 2007

Acknowledgments

Writing this book has been a remarkably enjoyable experience, facilitated by the cooperation, assistance, and encouragement of a number of colleagues and friends. The first expression of gratitude goes to Dr. Priscilla Ferguson Clement, Professor Emerita of History at Penn State University, and Elizabeth Potenza of Praeger Publishers. I greatly appreciated their kind invitation to contribute to Praeger's important series on the history of childhood in the United States and their patience with me throughout the writing process, which as might be expected has been fraught with unexpected obstacles and opportunities. Professor Clement has served admirably and with great dedication as the primary editor of this work; it is a much better book because of her skill and critique. Ms. Potenza has been gracious and cooperative throughout an extended period of research and writing, providing me with a freedom of thought and expression that has been as liberating as it has been valued. Of course, any errors of fact or judgment are mine and mine alone. I also wish to thank David Braddock and Laura Haffer of the Archives of the Coleman Institute for Cognitive Disabilities at the University of Colorado at Boulder. They provided wonderful access and advice during two extended periods of research for both this book and my previous book, *The History of Inclusion in the United States*. Their accommodating library and cordial colleagues made my time in Colorado especially memorable.

    I would like to extend my warmest gratitude to my wonderful friends and colleagues at the Indiana University School of Education at IUPUI. Khaula Murtadha, Deborah and Greg Keller, Rob Helfenbein, Charlie Barman, Jeff Anderson, and Mary Jo Dare have been especially helpful and encouraging throughout this process of writing and reflection; their interest in this project has been especially comforting and important to me. And I certainly wish to thank my Indiana family: my wife Elisabeth, my children Evan and Laurel, and my mother-in-law Pearl Hinshaw. This book would not have been possible without their love and support. Finally, this book is dedicated to the memory of my mother, Mary Anne Daugherty Osgood, who shared my love of history but passed away before having the chance to read this.

Indianapolis, Indiana
May 2007

Introduction

They have gathered and learned in places as diverse and as ordinary as one could imagine. They have met in homes and in church basements and other informal settings, in imposing buildings of astounding size and architecture, in portable classrooms on the outskirts of school playgrounds, in anonymous locations known only to those involved, and in everyday schoolrooms in the neighborhood public school. Their experiences in these settings have been even more varied than the places themselves, differentiated by purpose, belief, social mores, economic conditions, and historical eras. Over time, the location of their schools and the education provided in them have moved much closer to the mainstream of schools and society. Nonetheless, many continue to experience their education and this world in fundamentally distinct and problematic ways.

Throughout our nation's history, children identified as disabled in the United States have lived lives reflecting a remarkable ambivalence toward their place in American society. Life as a "person with a disability" has dramatically defined the extent of such children's visibility, status, and opportunity among the nation's citizenry. As part of Praeger's series Growing Up: History of Children and Youth, *The History of Special Education* takes an extended look at how these children, their families, and others important to them have constructed and interpreted their lives. While the primary focus will be on disabled children's experiences in schools and other educational settings, the relation of their formal education to the rest of their lives in the home and community will also be discussed.

The transition of special education and disability services from being an almost exclusively private venture two hundred years ago to being a central component of public initiatives and interests reflects the United States' growing awareness of the extent of disability in this country and the importance of the fundamental civil and human rights of those labeled as disabled. For hundreds of years, American society has joined the rest of the world in identifying and constructing various manifestations of disability and has developed specific policies and practices toward those it has so labeled. As a result, the history of special education in this country is long and complex, rooted in controversy and rich in human stories. This volume is situated in both established as well as recent developments in research in the history of special education and in the growing field of disability studies. It also draws on the extensive body of professional and personal literature exploring disability as a personal characteristic, as a unique identifier of certain collective communities, and as a defining feature of educational and social experience.

Central to the book's documentary evidence are official school and institutional records: annual reports, reports of directors or superintendents, special field reports of particular programs, commissioned school system surveys, and newsletters. It also draws significantly on articles in professional journals and popular print media, including featured articles and letters in magazines and newspapers. Local, state, and federal government documents provide a rich source of information, as do the published testimonials in both article and book form written by persons whose lives have been directly affected by disability. Organizations and associations formed to advocate on behalf of persons with disabilities also have published a great deal of material describing their lives in home, school, and community. Among the richest are those of the Arc, the national advocacy group that seeks to represent the interests of persons with cognitive disabilities. (These files may be found at the Archives of the Coleman Institute for Cognitive Disabilities, housed at the University of Colorado at Boulder.)

This history focuses less on laws, policies, structures, and operations of special education and more on the lived experiences of those involved as they were shaped by these external forces. The landscape of such experiences covers considerable territory: public and private segregated institutions, public school systems, with segregated as well as fully inclusive settings, and other settings such as social agencies, hospitals, private specialized schools, and homes.

In earlier times, settings such as almshouses, county poorhouses, and even prisons also served as quasi-permanent settings for disabled individuals, either by intention or default. Such places come alive through the words, depictions, photographs, and narratives of those who have experienced them directly. It is this volume's goal to capture and present that record in a clear, organized, and instructive form.

ORGANIZATION

The structure of the book follows a general chronological framework, tracing consistent and recurring themes, topics, and issues related to the lives of children with disabilities in schools, institutions, and families. Chapter 1 provides an overview of important developments in American social and intellectual history that had a direct bearing on the lives of children, including children with disabilities. It discusses how the sweeping nineteenth-century processes of urbanization, industrialization, immigration, and progressivist thought transformed the lives of all children and their families. The United States became a vastly different nation between 1800 and 1900, and this chapter explains how the country changed and how those changes led to new modes and models of life for persons with disabilities. This chapter also describes how policies and practices related to disability among children evolved. It examines the various ways in which state and local governments responded to the heightened visibility of and concern about disability in their jurisdictions. The chapter details the creation of an array of special education programs in large urban public school systems, and the accommodations of special needs among students in rural schools. It also briefly explains the origins of private and public institutions for children with disabilities.

Chapters 2 and 3 cover the growth of institutions and special education programs in considerably greater detail. Chapter 2 traces the development of the mission, structure, and characteristics of residential institutions for the disabled, emphasizing those for the mentally disabled but also discussing those for the deaf and for the blind. Chapter 3 covers a wide range of topics and issues concerning the origins and development of special education in the public schools and their impact on school children identified as disabled until just before the Second World War. Chapter 4 looks at the period of 1940 to 1960, a time when public school special education programs became more entrenched, residential institutions experienced rapid growth and increasing criticism, and the American public gained greater exposure to issues of disability and the presence of the disabled in society. Chapter 5 then examines the years between 1960 and 1980. This was a key transitional period in the lives of children with disabilities, during which a series of fundamental changes in policy and practice regarding disability profoundly altered the ways in which disabled children were identified and their needs addressed in institutions, schools, and communities. Chapter 6 concludes the book by reviewing the more than 150 years of this history and identifying key themes and characteristics that despite so many changes, it is argued, continue to define the lives of children identified as disabled.

WHY THIS STORY?

A history of the lives of children living with disability contributes to a more authentic and enriched understanding of *all* children. Children with disabilities have always been present in this country, and their presence has had a profound effect on educational and public policies that have in turn affected the lives and belief systems of all children.

Furthermore, a history of the experiences of children with disabilities allows us to understand the important ethical questions that arise from our definitions of the social roles and status of children who have been seen as "crippled," "defective," "deficient," "subnormal," or "handicapped." Do they deserve less or more attention than others? Do they merit receiving more or less money, space, time, and material drawn from a limited supply of resources? Finally, how have children who are disabled stood as a priority for families, schools, governments, businesses, and health and social services?

EMERGENT THEMES

Arguably the most important outcome of historical research is a richer and more sophisticated understanding of the present: we learn about how events in the past may have set the stage for today's assumptions and practices in a given field or arena. This particular study allows us to understand the historical experiences of children directly and indirectly affected by the presence of disability in family, school, and society. In doing so, we can identify as well as grapple with certain questions and themes that have remained consistent features of these experiences over time up to the present day. These include the following:

- In what ways, and to what extent, have children with disabilities experienced *acceptance* or *rejection* by and among the American public?

- What *practical concerns* have characterized the structuring of the daily lives of disabled children?

- Which *political and ideological perspectives* have been particularly influential in shaping the lives of disabled children in schools and communities?

- How have *emerging notions of ethics and human rights* shaped policy and practice regarding disability among children in the United States?

- In what ways, and to what extent, have the *status and reputation* of those directly involved in working with disabled children in the United States changed over time?

Readers should know at the outset that these themes and issues arise constantly and in many forms throughout this history and thus are crucial to discussing disability among children from historical and current perspectives.

LIMITATIONS AND PARAMETERS OF THE STUDY

For a history of children with disabilities, the public and private records offer but a limited glimpse into their lives. Many of those who created these records were persons who had only a partial understanding of the context and meaning of what they described. Especially for the nineteenth and early twentieth centuries, the marginalized status of special education and of institutions for the disabled means that historians must exercise great care and take interpretive risks in using the available evidence to explain and justify their particular view of the lives involved.

Since the mid–twentieth century, evidence from those more directly involved has become more voluminous and readily available. Documents and reports have become more accessible to the public even as the public itself has shown greater interest in the lives of these children and of those who have worked with them. The voices of persons with disabilities have gained a much wider audience and are viewed with greater credibility and care. The expansion of professional literature on disability and the movement on several fronts to strengthen and ensure the civil and human rights of persons with disabilities have generated a considerable flow of rich, realistic, and informative historical evidence. While a truly complete national investigation of this topic would take many decades and innumerable careers to accomplish, a determined and careful examination of authentically representative data can lead to a plausible and informative interpretation of the past. That is what this volume has attempted to do.

Use of the construct of disability itself also has its limitations. Understandings of what "disability" truly is have shifted with the passage of time. As this history shows, notions about the nature of disability and of those who exhibited it have transformed from the simplistic, uncertain, and thus vague ideas of the 1800s to highly specialized, often clinical, and science-based definitions of the early 2000s. Our appreciation of just how complex an entity disability is has grown dramatically. Our realization of its linkages to other social, medical, and cognitive conditions has been as enlightening as it has been overwhelming. For the purposes of this volume, disability refers to those *personal, cognitive, physical, and behavioral* conditions that have been identified as significantly limiting an individual's ability to function effectively in normal societal situations: family, neighborhood, school, and workplace. Its focus is on children who have been labeled disabled, either formally by professionals or informally—yet with considerable confidence—by family members, employers, teachers, and others who have a role in determining a child's life pathways.

Such an approach certainly risks defining children too narrowly by their disabling condition or conditions. Issues of race, ethnicity, class, and gender become obfuscated when disability serves as the primary, if not exclusive, lens through which we consider these children. Interestingly, most of the literature discussing disability remains silent on these other features of a child's life: the focus is on their disability and their struggles, frustrations, and accomplishments that result from that condition. This volume thus focuses almost exclusively on disability as a child's defining construct, with significant attention also given to a child's socioeconomic status. This is not to say, however, that differences among the experiences of disabled children are never a function of these other crucial constructs. The interactions of race, ethnicity, and gender with disability offer the opportunity for more specialized and focused scholarship in the history of disability that extends well beyond the scope of this introductory volume. Institutions and schools for disabled children that are segregated by race and/or gender, for example, may yield individual records and documents that allow a more detailed examination of potential subtle, substantial, and certainly real differences among experiences that can help move the history of childhood and disability further ahead.

Finally, this history, as with all histories, is shaped by the particular positioning and agency of the author. As one who has been directly involved in the lives of children with identified disabilities as a teacher, parent, family member, and advocate, I readily acknowledge my support for efforts to improve the lives of these children and my impatience with those who attempt to minimize their potential or trivialize their accomplishments. Nevertheless I also recognize that as a historian it is my obligation and certainly my goal to present a balanced, fair, and comprehensive history that respects views different from my own and recognizes that there are multiple ways to define and interpret the propriety of particular policies, practices, and perspectives. I invite the reader to join in this journey and reach her or his own conclusions.

The Changing Worlds of American Children, 1800–1940

> The child lives in a somewhat narrow world of personal contacts. Things hardly come within his experience unless they touch, intimately and obviously, his own well-being, or that of his family and friends. His world is a world of persons with their personal interests, rather than a realm of facts and laws. Not truth, in the sense of conformity to external fact, but affection and sympathy, is its keynote.
>
> —John Dewey, *The Child and the Curriculum* (1902)[1]

This view of childhood, offered by one of the most dedicated and respected supporters of child-centered education in American history, presents a striking contrast to the immense complexity and energy that characterized the United States at the turn of the twentieth century. Dewey's view of the child's world as something intimate, simple, and personal appears to have been completely out of place in a country that had grown tremendously in size, diversity, economic muscle, and worldwide political influence over the previous one hundred years. Moreover, the environments in which children found themselves, and the assumptions regarding the nature of childhood itself, had undergone similar and equally dramatic transformations over the same period.

Yet Dewey's view is crucial to appreciating the necessity of exploring a child's world through a child's lens, especially considering how much the condition of disability could and did affect the daily experiences of a child's life, then as now. This chapter provides a broad overview of those sweeping changes during the nineteenth and early twentieth centuries that established the general social and intellectual landscape, changes that shaped the lives of every American at the time. For children with disabilities, these transformations fundamentally affected their interactions with government agencies, public schools, and private initiatives dedicated to addressing disability in society. Nevertheless, most disabled children knew little of this context. Instead, their world was defined much more by how teachers, public officials, parents, friends, classmates, and strangers talked and reacted to them; how the structures in their lives (schools, institutions, agencies) often isolated them from others; and how doctors and other specialists confronted them with questions, tests, physical exams, and comments that invaded their deeply personal world and often demonstrated a terrible lack of "affection and sympathy." Amid profound social evolution, every child with a disability experienced a unique existence, at once shaped by forces beyond their imagination as well as by those that played constant, intimate roles in their lives. This chapter establishes the context for this informative and important paradox.

THE UNITED STATES IN TRANSFORMATION

The United States of 1800 looked and felt vastly different than it would in 1900. In 1800, the new nation was very young and was just developing a national identity. Local, often isolated communities constituted the primary boundaries of life and influence for the great majority of people. Except for a few notable and sizable urban centers, the country was overwhelmingly rural in character, agrarian in economic activity, and parochial in its worldview. Even though the U.S. population itself came from a multitude of ethnic and racial backgrounds, local communities tended to be homogenous in language, religion, and interests.[2]

The lives of children reflected these conditions. Their worlds were indeed limited and small, with families (either natural or "adopted" through apprenticeship) their centerpiece. Formal schooling reached relatively few children and varied considerably in form and content depending on geographic location. The lives of most children included some form of work, either on the family farm, in the master's shop, or in the family trade or business. Once a child reached the age of seven to ten years, childhood itself was usually left behind and the youngster assumed a more adult role in the community.[3]

Throughout the 1800s, the United States experienced social and economic changes on a massive scale. Historians of nineteenth-century America offer many alternative explanations of how and why these changes occurred, but most agree that the processes of urbanization, industrialization, and immigration strongly influenced nineteenth-century history. Inextricably linked, these processes produced seismic shifts in the social and economic structure of the country. As a result, throughout the young nation, the lives of literally millions of individuals, their families, and their communities underwent profound and permanent changes. American children experienced these changes not only as family and community members but also as key actors and agents in the process of transformation itself. Their roles in this dramatically evolving country proved to be as vital as they were varied.

The movement of large numbers of persons from rural to urban areas commenced in earnest early in the nineteenth century. Larger cities in the United States grew steadily as a result of migration from countryside to city as well as from an influx of people from outside the United States—especially Canada and northern Europe. Locations such as Boston, New York, Philadelphia, and Baltimore attracted individuals and families looking for opportunities and personal enrichment in the form of work, culture, education, money, and possibility. These proved to be powerful magnets for people seeking better lives. Larger and more concentrated population centers continued to develop and increase in number as the century went on, leading to the tremendous range of social and economic advances and problems that beset a significantly urban United States by the early 1900s.[4]

Coupled closely with urbanization was the transformation of the national economy from an almost exclusively agrarian to a substantially industrial one. With more concentrated populations in cities and with truly remarkable developments in technology, industry became more efficient and responsive to changing market demands. The ready availability of workers, including women and children, provided the labor force. The growing national population and increasing public wealth fueled the demand. While farming and other agricultural pursuits remained an important sector of the American economy—especially as the nation and much of its population continued to move westward—industrial productivity became a hallmark of American power. Urban life and an industrial economy had become key features of the United States by the early twentieth century, helping to define the American experience in fundamental ways.[5]

Also fueling these dramatic transformations was the immigration of millions of persons to the United States from other parts of the world. Individuals

and families from Canada, China, and all over Europe relocated to the United
States in near-unimaginable numbers. Migration to the North American con-
tinent had, of course, occurred for centuries, but its rapid and highly controversial increase in the United States during the 1800s (especially in the 1830s and
1840s and from 1880 to World War I) overshadowed considerably those earlier
numbers. Exploration, slavery, and indentured servitude had brought sizable
numbers of workers during the colonial and early national eras. However, the
waves of immigration to the east and west coasts during the later nineteenth
and early twentieth centuries consisted mostly of individuals and families pur-
suing the promise—real or imagined—that life in the young nation seemed to
offer those who left their homelands for economic, political, legal, religious,
or personal reasons. Immigrants settled in cities large and small as well as
in rural areas in the mid and far western sections of the United States. They
provided an easy supply of cheap labor for industry and millions of workers
on farms and in local communities. Their presence and influence made for
national achievements as well as national challenges as the diverse cultural,
linguistic, religious, and political characteristics of immigrants created both
rich opportunity and tremendous conflict.[6]

These drastic transformations had profound implications for the lives and
futures of children in the United States. Traditions such as apprenticeship and
working in home or on the family farm slowly but surely began to disappear.
Much larger numbers of children found themselves living in urban environments and working for industrial concerns. Children also participated in piece-
rate manufacturing with their families or found other modes of livelihood—
legal and illicit—on city streets. School attendance became a more popular and
socially sanctioned (as well as required) option. The experiences of children
varied widely depending on age, gender, race, social class, location, and cultural
background. Indeed, to speak of a generic American childhood experience is
misleading and unhelpful. As historian Joseph Illick notes, every American
child experienced childhood in unique ways based on who they were, where
they lived, and what their families did and believed. What was common, however, was that these worlds of childhood bore but limited resemblance to the
worlds of childhood before 1800.[7]

EXTERNAL INFLUENCES ON THE LIVES OF CHILDREN

With the dramatic increase in the numbers of persons in the United States
living and working in urban environments, the problems that nearly always

accompany urban life multiplied. Concentrated populations of available labor led directly to lower wages and heightened competition for paying jobs. Rapid growth of and little disposable income among newcomers to the cities contributed to overcrowded and decrepit living conditions for millions. Rates of poverty and crime grew, and public as well as personal health problems multiplied. Children, who made up a considerable portion of the urban population, often found themselves working in near-intolerable conditions for little pay. Many sought income from a wide range of activities in their neighborhoods, as whatever income they generated went to support their families. Their high visibility and frequent forays into crime, petty, or otherwise, greatly disturbed the urban citizens and leaders. Reform movements to correct urban and other social ills highlighted much of the social and intellectual activity at different times during the 1800s. Efforts to end slavery, eradicate poverty, cure alcoholism, encourage spiritual awakening, advance patriotism, expand educational opportunity, enhance opportunities for women and children, and improve the physical and mental health of urban populations began early in the century and continued well into the next. The commitment to reform persisted even as targets of reform efforts shifted.[8]

One vitally important and sweeping response to the problems of urbanization, industrialization, and immigration came in the Progressive Era, usually defined as the period 1880–1920. As it applied to urban life, Progressivism called for efficiency in government, serious attention to issues of public welfare, and active intervention in private lives in ways that would alter individual behavior and hopefully benefit the public sphere. Progressive civic leaders considered it their duty to identify problems—individual as well as societal—and take proactive measures that may well have entrenched their positions of authority and social control but would nonetheless demonstrate their commitment to social betterment. While individual freedom was still valued during the Progressive Era, local and state governments saw it as their responsibility to enact policy that ensured social progress even if it placed previously nonexistent limits on the lives and choices of individuals, families, or small communities. The result was a significantly expanded role for government in the name of progress. Traditional dependence on local control eroded as large city as well as state governments established policies, regulations, and institutions that manifested what were considered legitimate and appropriate interests and responsibilities of the public sphere in a progressive United States. Certainly, these governmental bodies had been expanding their realms of influence for decades in certain areas such as education. However, the

Progressive Era accelerated that process and solidified the expanding role of government in the lives of citizens.[9]

This expansion of government interest manifested itself in a variety of ways, many of which directly affected the lives of children. Legislation addressing issues such as child labor, truancy, vagrancy, poverty, and compulsory education became increasingly common as the nineteenth century progressed. For example, the state of Massachusetts, which had taken a leadership role in advancing state involvement in public education, passed a series of laws addressing child labor and compulsory education. These laws placed previously unheard-of restrictions on what families and employers could determine for children in terms of working hours, working conditions, and school attendance.[10]

Legislation regarding public schooling constituted a central feature of nineteenth-century reform. Throughout the 1800s, states claimed more and more supervisory responsibility over not just the schools themselves but also the children who were expected to attend them. Massachusetts led the way: it established the first state Board of Education in 1837 and enacted the nation's first true compulsory education law in 1852. By 1900, most states had done the same, with Board powers frequently being enhanced and compulsory education laws expanded and strengthened over time. Because of the diversification of the nation's population and the mass concentration of immigrant populations in cities, schools were charged to assume a greater role as social service and acculturation agencies. The nation's schoolhouses, many argued, had to take the lead in guiding children from all kinds of backgrounds down paths that ensured public safety, economic stability, and cultural integrity. Moreover, the changing face of the nation required purposeful, publicly supported policies and initiatives that would ensure its future and protect its people. Significantly, the presence of persons with disability in society—a presence viewed as growing larger and more dangerous as time went on—drew the attention of those promoting and making such policies and altered the landscape of the lives of the disabled permanently and fundamentally.[11]

DISABILITY AND THE PUBLIC SPHERE

Societies have acknowledged the existence of disability for thousands of years. Depending on the era and the culture, persons with significant and obvious disabling conditions have been demonized, deified, ignored, persecuted, protected, or isolated and exterminated. In the colonial and early national eras of the United States, persons with disabilities either were kept at home, tolerated and even supported by communities, or expelled, prosecuted, and even condemned. Before the early nineteenth century, the deaf, the blind, the physically crippled, and those with various vaguely defined yet obvious forms of mental incapacity constituted the visible, and thus recognized, population of persons with disabilities. Public policies such as "warning out" (a method of excluding nonresident poor from local communities), institutions such as the colonial mental hospital in Williamsburg, VA, and private efforts of persons such as Thomas Gallaudet and Samuel Gridley Howe represented different approaches to addressing disability. By 1850, a few notable initiatives had occurred. The Asylum for the Deaf in Hartford, CT, opened in 1817 after Gallaudet traveled to Europe to learn teaching methods for the deaf and recruit teachers as well as obtain financial support. Largely through Howe's efforts, an Asylum for the Blind and another for Idiotic and Feeble-minded Youth opened in Massachusetts in 1832 and 1848, respectively. Furthermore, Howe's widely publicized and celebrated successful teaching of deaf–blind child Laura Bridgman in the 1830s helped generate much greater optimism in the ability to teach children with severe disabilities. Interest in institutionalizing, educating, treating, and even curing persons with disabilities thus grew steadily as the century progressed.[12]

These developments unfolded in conjunction with the widespread changes affecting the young United States noted earlier. Concentrated city populations magnified the visibility of and concern about disabled persons. At the same time, the perceived need for greater control over individuals and social groups—especially of poor and/or immigrant populations—grew. With far greater numbers of people employed in large enterprises such as factories and mills, and fewer working in homes or small neighborhoods, individual behavior and capability became more important. So did the ability to function effectively in a collective workplace environment. Moreover, the growth of the number of schools and students, especially in urban areas, demanded increased structure, stratification, and standardization in classrooms and among schools within school districts. As schools became more rigid, abnormal student performance and behavior stood out. Teachers and administrators now saw conditions among children that previously went unnoticed or that had been managed with greater flexibility. Attention to the nature and extent of individual differences, especially those that affected the ability to function successfully in society, increased. Thus by 1900, disability had become a key construct and target for progressive reformers.

With heightened awareness came an increasingly cautious and pessimistic view of disability. By the early 1900s, the state of being disabled generated considerable suspicion, even outright contempt, among many. Doctors, teachers, institution and school administrators, and researchers in the burgeoning field of "feeblemindedness" or "mental deficiency" employed a variety of allegedly scientific and objective means to establish the hereditary and malevolent nature of this condition. In the early twentieth century, "mental deficiency" assumed a much more widespread and dangerous status than had been the case four or five decades earlier. After 1870, both public and private institutions for the disabled focused less on treatment, education, and cure and more on isolation, custodial care, and eradication. In addition, school systems in the larger cities began developing segregated programs for children considered disabled. Reformers argued that they were attending to both the individual needs of disabled students and the general welfare and protection of the "normal" student population. Using more complex and arguably more sophisticated methods of identification, administrators assigned larger numbers of children in urban public schools to "special" settings where they could exist isolated from the mainstream and have less of an impact on the operation of schools.[13]

THE EVOLUTION OF DISABILITY POLICY AND PRACTICE

In 1853, Samuel Gridley Howe, noted social reformer in Massachusetts and pioneer in American special education, identified "institutions for the blind, deaf, and dumb, and for the feeble-minded . . . [as] links in the chain of common schools—the last indeed, but still a necessary link in order to embrace all the children in the State." Howe's reasoning helped convince the Massachusetts state legislature to support the first public institution for "feebleminded" individuals in the country and underscored the need to address the presence of disability among children. Nationwide, institutions for the disabled became more numerous and more crowded as efforts to identify and treat persons with disabilities gained greater momentum. Concurrently, public schools officials, especially in urban areas, more commonly acknowledged disability among students. With powerful social forces transforming the child's world in the United States and children themselves becoming the subjects of increased concern and scrutiny, the late 1800s and the early 1900s challenged children and those who worked with them to adjust to dramatically new assumptions and conditions.[14]

Looking at Children and Disability Differently

In the late eighteenth century, European educators such as Jean-Jacques Rousseau and Johann Pestalozzi had argued for educational settings for children that respected their interests and emphasized positive, individualized attention. The result was that respect for a child's individual differences in learning and behavior gained some credence, as evidenced in more careful study of children and in the development of individual approaches to learning for children who clearly needed them. Rousseau's and Pestalozzi's work came to the United States relatively early in the nineteenth century, spread by reformers such as Howe, Calvin Stowe, John Griscom, Enoch Cobb Wines, and Horace Mann. Their notions of child-centered education suited emerging American sensibilities regarding the significance of childhood and the importance of a more nurturing approach to teaching. Potential beneficiaries of a child-centered approach were children with visible and significant disabilities. Personalized, one-on-one instruction had long represented a hallmark of the education of deaf persons and blind persons. In 1848, noted educator Eduoard Seguin brought his "physiological method" for teaching individual children with severe mental disabilities to the United States. It became the cornerstone of early formal education efforts in this nation's first institutions for the mentally disabled.[15]

Throughout the nineteenth century, the trend to view children as unique individuals in strong need of nurturing combined with a heightened academic interest in children helped sow the seeds of the child study movement. One of this movement's leading advocates, psychologist G. Stanley Hall, drew nationwide attention with his theories on the unique nature of childhood and adolescence. Consequently, educators, doctors, and other psychologists linked psychological studies of the child with educational theories that focused on children and their need for a supportive learning environment at home and school. Child study drew on these and other apparently successful attempts to demonstrate the value of individualized attention to children. By the late nineteenth century, even tradition-bound public school officials were calling for individualized instruction of disabled students.[16]

Changing Worlds of Children: The Urban Public School

The remarkable growth of public education in most regions of the United States is one of the most important stories of the nineteenth century.

During this common school movement in the 1800s, schools transformed from small, highly localized spaces that focused on basic literacy skills and religious training to more complex systems that served a wide range of students and provided multiple services. This change was especially apparent in larger cities, where school buildings contained multiple classrooms and became centers of social activity and important, highly visible features of neighborhoods. School assumed a more central place in the lives of most children, at least for a good portion of their childhood.

The city of Boston, Massachusetts, offered an excellent representative example of how and why these urban school systems developed. The city's public school system had been established in 1789. However, it became more directly involved in the lives of much larger numbers of children when it added primary schools for boys and girls ages four through seven in 1818. By 1820, the city's leaders had already expressed great alarm at the number of "urchins" roaming Boston's streets, most of whom were believed to come from poor, mostly immigrant families. Claiming that sending such children to school would solve the problem of child homelessness, the city leaders strengthened truancy enforcement even before the enactment of a compulsory education law. In 1836, the state passed legislation prohibiting employment for children younger than fifteen who had not been enrolled in school for three months prior to beginning work. In 1838, the school system established a system of "Intermediate Schools," also known as "Schools for Special Instruction," whose purpose was to provide a segregated setting for older immigrant children who needed to learn to read and write in English. Within a decade, these school settings held more than 13 percent of all of Boston's schoolchildren. In 1852, Massachusetts enacted the nation's first compulsory education law. Although modest in scope and weak in enforcement, the law manifested the state's and city's desire to place children in public schools.[17]

Boston also took national leadership in formalizing structures and standardizing practices for public school systems. City officials implemented graded instruction (i.e., placing students in classes based on chronological age) in 1847 and worked hard to standardize the curriculum for all schools. A major reorganization and streamlining of the Boston School Committee in 1876, and another in 1905, exemplified the rapid growth and increased complexity of the system itself. Throughout the later 1800s, the state continually strengthened its compulsory education laws, bringing more and more children into the city's schools for longer periods of time. System administration also expanded as assistant superintendents and directors of various offices were added to the organization charts. By the early 1900s, Boston had over 80,000 children enrolled in its public schools (a majority of whom were either born overseas or born to immigrant parents in the United States), and the Boston public schools displayed a remarkable degree of complexity.[18]

Furthermore, Boston served as an excellent example of how changing urban landscapes, progressive ideas, a focus on individual children, and a heightened awareness of disabling conditions among children combined to create special education. In 1879, the Boston School Committee transformed the system's intermediate schools into "ungraded classes," which, although designated for older children who were learning to read and write, soon became de facto settings—or "dumping grounds"—for students who were struggling academ- ically or behaviorally in regular classrooms. For nearly twenty years, these classes acted as safety valves for an increasingly stratified and rigid school system, one that was designed for lockstep, uniform performance but concur- rently faced the harsh reality of widely divergent cultures, backgrounds, needs, abilities, and interests among its students.[19]

Around the turn of the century, Boston began establishing more and more such segregated settings, only these were tailored to specific conditions or needs of students. In 1869, the city established a public day school for deaf students. In 1895, Boston started a Parental School for truants and other transgressors, which became the Disciplinary Day School in 1915. In 1899, the Boston public schools opened its first class for students identified as "mentally deficient." Within the next fifteen years, specialized classes and programs for children with chronic illnesses, vision impairments, speech disorders, giftedness, and low English proficiency were created in the school system. By the 1920s, special education stood as an established aspect of public schools in the city, with over 5 percent of children enrolled in a designated specialized setting.[20]

Boston was by no means alone among cities in the United States in creat- ing and developing special education programs for children with disabilities. By the first decade of the twentieth century, Chicago, New York, Cleveland, Baltimore, Philadelphia, and Los Angeles, among others, had taken similar approaches to accommodating students with disabilities. By the 1920s, "spe- cial classes" for children with mental retardation were standard in most large school systems and in some smaller cities. The National Education Association (NEA) formed a Department of Special Education shortly after 1900 to pro- vide opportunities to exchange ideas, information, and best practices among those involved in special education activities. The *NEA Proceedings* and other professional journals such as *Training School Bulletin, Ungraded,* and the *Journal of Psycho-Asthenics* offered forums for articles on research and teaching strategies for children with disabilities. By 1930 in the United States, special education in urban public schools had become a standard feature of public education. Special education now directly affected the lives of hundreds of thousands of children across the country.[21]

Changing Worlds of Children: The Rural School

Schools in small-town or rural settings in the United States presented a stark contrast to those in urban areas. Rural educators still held deep attachments to the notion of strictly local control of almost every aspect of schooling, from funding and hiring to curriculum development, recordkeeping, and teacher training. Most rural schools were small and offered limited hours both in terms of the school day and the school year. They relied on local resources and expectations to develop and implement instruction; they practiced multiage and multigrade grouping in individual classrooms. Often one teacher of one class constituted the entire school. There was also typically a high turnover among teachers as well as students, so that stability in schooling from year to year—and even month to month—proved tenuous at best. Classes varied greatly in size, and student attendance was inconsistent.[22]

Given these conditions, it is no surprise that formal identification of children with disabilities and special education programs to meet their learning needs were limited in rural or other small districts. In most of these schools, which usually covered only elementary grades, instruction concentrated on basic skills. Most teachers adapted instruction individually to each child, not just to those with clear learning "problems." Until the 1900s, the structural and operational pressures that led larger urban school systems to develop special education programs did not exist in one-room schoolhouses and one-school districts in small-town and rural America. Rural schools also lacked the professional staff to determine specific disabling conditions among children. Disabled youngsters either functioned in school, stopped attending, or never attended at all. Weak enforcement of compulsory education laws in rural areas where formal schooling seemed less a need and more a luxury was typical, as was the absence of preparing teachers to work with disabled students. Children with unusually significant disabilities therefore usually stayed at home to learn and work or found occupations that did not require formal schooling.

Although rural educators noted certain kinds of disability (as will be discussed in Chapter 3), rural children who exhibited significant limitations in cognitive, physical, or behavioral functioning typically spent most of their time in places other than school.

Changing Worlds of Children: Public and Private Institutions

Those "other places" included the child's home or a local institution designed to serve needy individuals and families. These institutions were by no means limited to rural areas. In large cities as well as in small towns, institutions such as county poor houses (or almshouses), county jails, mental hospitals, orphanages, or other agencies for destitute, incapacitated, or otherwise dependent persons often housed individuals with disabilities. Many of these were children. As the next chapter will document, the presence of disabled persons in institutions that were not designed to accommodate or treat them became a growing concern in the Progressive Era. Ultimately, their presence led to deliberate efforts to relocate children and others into environments more tailored to them as persons with disabilities.

Public and private institutions for the disabled, which also accommodated children, grew in number in the nineteenth century. Before 1850, only a handful of such places existed, most in the Northeast and almost all designed to treat deaf, blind, or "feebleminded" persons. Usually, persons with different disabilities were treated in separate facilities but sometimes all were cared for under one roof. Between 1850 and 1900, the number of such institutions increased dramatically as state governments entered the business of identifying, segregating, and treating individuals with disabilities of all ages. This growth occurred from coast to coast and paralleled medical, educational, and social developments in the understanding and treatment of disability. Such institutions usually opened with the noble goal of educating and perhaps even curing their charges. Eventually, however, asylums for the disabled helped perpetuate the transition noted earlier from cautious optimism to heightened skepticism and contempt regarding disability and the disabled individual. The superintendents, directors, and other administrative leaders of these institutions worked with state governments to build these facilities and then shape their programs and missions in ways that supported the states' concerns about disability in the population. As of the early twentieth century, such institutions were firmly entrenched not only in state budgets but also in the minds and plans of social reformers.[23]

Disability and the Home: Childhood and Family Life

The proper role and function of children in society constituted a subject of sustained debate well into the 1900s as large numbers of children—despite strengthened compulsory education laws—stayed away from school, either to work as paid employees of companies or to otherwise help generate income for their families (via a variety of licit and illicit means). The debate was important because at its heart rested a basic question: to what extent can the public, through laws and government, dictate or direct the lives of minors? Progressive social reformers expressed great concern over the "wayward" attractions of life outside home and school for children, especially those from impoverished urban neighborhoods. Children's undesirable activities on the streets disturbed the civic and religious leadership just as much in 1930 as in 1830, and the call for governments to intervene grew louder as time passed.

The concept of government's ultimate right to tell individuals and families what to do with their children in order to improve society carried over easily into the world of disability. Until the establishment of school programs and residential institutions for the disabled, the family or small community had served as primary caretakers for individuals whose disabilities required significant attention and support. Given the relative absence of understanding of disabling conditions—especially mental disability—at the time and many suspicions about their origins and meaning, families and communities often struggled terribly to provide that support and care. Indeed, a primary rationale for establishing residential institutions was to relieve families and communities of the "grievous burden" of housing a disabled child or adult.[24]

State involvement and eventual control of policies and operations for persons with disability intensified as concern grew about the increasing presence of indigent "feebleminded" persons in county poorhouses and the emerging contempt for their mental condition. "This class of unfortunates," wrote Indiana educator Harriet Foster, "thrill us with horror and disgust with their repulsive looks and loathsome manners. They are shunned by men, kept in the dark corners of the world, and looked upon with shame and loathing by their natural protectors." As early as 1879, Foster had argued forcefully for the state to step in and establish an institution to take them away from long-suffering families and overwhelmed county institutions. "There are cases known where the unremitting care of an imbecile child has sent the mother to an early grave. Other cases are known also where the burden of such a being has reduced entire families to pauperism . . . [they need] a variety of requirements that can only be maintained by a State government." Foster cited other states that had taken this necessary step.[25]

By the early 1900s, state worries over the family's role in the life of a child with a disability had expanded to consider the alleged hereditary nature of mental defect and other disabilities. Concern also arose over the ways in which a family's social and economic status as well as home environment contributed directly to the negative impact of disability on society. Ida Gregory of the Juvenile Court in Denver wrote that "the American home is the bulwark of the nation, the Rock of Ages, the tie that binds us together." While she argued that "the right of parents must be conserved," she also noted that "their economic problems are serious and we must never forget our solemn obligations to the helpless and the unfortunate." That home life—of whatever quality—had a tremendous impact on children and on their future constituted a fundamental tenet of public policy and social reform at the time. A school superintendent from Brooklyn, New York, expressed this sentiment thusly:

> Among the educational factors making for the development of character and mind . . . the family stands out prominent. The first school that a human being enters is the home. Its lessons are well taught and well learned. . . . It is in the schoolroom of the home that a person starts on the upward path leading to that expression of the better elements of his make-up which we know as education. . . . The pity of life is that not all homes work for this noble end.

The official went on to say that poverty, immorality, and unsanitary conditions make the home life of some families close to intolerable, commenting that "there is to be noted a peculiar leakage of home influences among our immigrants."[26]

The nature of home life and families beset with disability drew particular attention and concern. The classic and nationally publicized family "histories" of the Jukes and the Kallikaks purported to demonstrate how feeble-mindedness was genetically caused and almost certainly would have a huge impact on future generations and the societies in which they would live. Similarly, dysfunctional families were thought to generate a range of other problems, especially for children in schools, such as miscreant behavior or speech and health disorders. Even deafness was seen by many, including Alexander Graham Bell and supporters of a more integrative approach to deaf education and lifestyle, as a disabling condition that merited attempts at eradication and greater control over family life.[27]

Consequently, families harboring disabled persons—especially children—became targets for a range of social policy and legal initiatives. Among the most sensational and widespread were the ethnographic "studies" conducted by various agencies regarding the prevalence and condition of families with disabled persons. The national Eugenics Records Office supported and consulted on many such studies. These were usually conducted on behalf of state or research agencies charged with determining the prevalence and status of the living conditions of these families and homes throughout the United States. These descriptive studies contained vivid, judgmental, and even inflammatory language detailing the alleged horrific conditions and characters found in these situations. Such studies intended to instigate extensive alarm about the presence of mental defect and other kinds of disabilities in the nation and challenge—or frighten—governments into taking corrective action.[28]

By the early 1900s, the family and home were both thus seen as fertile territory for the perpetuation of disability. A social worker offered the following description of what she claimed was a common sight in her work:

> We are accustomed to looking at the relation of the feeble-minded and other defectives to the home from one angle, that is, what they mean to the home. We must all agree that, great as the cost of mental defectives to the state, the burden is heaviest upon the home, where it is, above all, a burden of sorrow....
>
> I can see the clumsy, deformed boy, unable to walk, dragging himself along the floor, looking at us with a sickening grin.
>
> I can see the feeble-minded mother, with her vacant stare, clasping in her arms her weazened baby, with its tiny head. The feeble-minded or insane mother is one of the most dreadful sights, and her "home" the most desolate of all, for she can neither keep house nor care for the children, and, of course, some of them inherit her defects.

After acknowledging that even wealthy families "are martyred to feeble-minded children," the author commented why she believed there existed a much stronger relationship between poverty and disability:

> It may help us to understand if we are able to imagine what would happen to our own selves, if *we* were reduced to abject poverty and wretchedness, if we were naked, cold, hungry, sick and miserable, amid distracting noises and horrid odors, unable to sleep for disturbance, with all the anxieties of poverty, and the cry of our children

for food we could not give them. How long would our bodies stand it, or morals, our religion—our minds? . . . What must it mean to be chained to an abhorrent environment, and have no respite of woods and fields, beauty and harmony, comfort and rest?[29]

Famed social worker Jane Addams also recognized the need to factor a family's home life into social services for children with disabilities. Addams joined others in her concern for families or parents that would resist appropriate services such as special education for their child. Addams insisted that trained professionals assigned to work with the home to support the "somewhat mentally deficient" or "incorrigible or delinquent" child usually managed to convince the parent that their "devotion" to their child should conquer any concerns they might have. "When deficient children are discovered in their homes," she wrote, "are taken care of by trained teachers, after they have been diagnosed by child-study departments, and when all the apparatus of public education is turned on, the parent is convinced that his child is not an exception. . . . The reaction of this change of attitude upon the entire family is something astonishing." Recognizing the complicated nature of problems in the home, others advocated careful and dedicated communication between the teacher in the school and the social workers, nurses, and/or court officers assigned to the family. Through such coordinated efforts, the state could become more successful in managing and improving these difficult situations on behalf of the children.[30]

Despite such optimism, tensions between the private home and the public sector persisted. For parents to acknowledge disability within the family was, as Jane Addams noted, often a difficult thing to do. Typical was this case from California regarding a mildly mentally disabled, "nonacademic" child:

"You can't put my Tony in the dumb-bell school." The irate mother spat the words out at the principal and the teacher who were trying to persuade her that her son would get the training he needed at the near-by Development School. She was the picture of outraged motherhood . . . who was making this fight for her beloved Tony. . . .

It is too bad the Development School is so misunderstood by parents and often by the teaching profession itself. . . . Sometimes it is even called the *dumb-bell* or *crazy* school. As a matter of fact, it is the school where the child of less than average intelligence is given his big opportunity.

The author, a special education teacher in the Los Angeles public school system, then contrasted this "Slavonian woman" with another mother: a wealthy,
"stately, well-dressed woman" she identified as "Mrs. Smith," whose family had
no history of mental defect. Mrs. Smith wished to place her child in the Development School as "she wants him to have the democratic training of the public
schools." The author concluded that "this story is one of a sensible woman
of courage who faces the fact that her son is below average intelligence. . . .
Her approach to the problem is scientific rather than emotional, and she is
doing all in her power to make his life happy and useful. . . . So we have the
two typically divergent attitudes. . . . Ignorance and superstition on the one
hand; knowledge and understanding on the other hand." Clearly, those in the
public sector—especially in the schools—had every confidence that families
would do well to listen to them and follow their advice. They expressed great
puzzlement that some families resisted their overtures so strongly.[31]

By the late 1930s, the United States thus had developed multiple ways for
addressing disability in society through public schools, public and private
institutions, and public policy. Children were central to these endeavors as the
nation's medical, educational, and intellectual leaders became convinced that
the eradication of disability depended on early identification, prevention, and
treatment. The next chapter takes a closer look at the residential institutions
for the disabled, the development of which reflected much about evolving
sensibilities regarding disability and the children who "had" it.

NOTES

1. John Dewey, *The School and Society/The Child and the Curriculum* (Chicago, IL,
1990), 183.

2. There are literally dozens of general social histories covering the United States
during the colonial and early national eras. One of the most accessible and convenient
is Allan Nevins and Henry Steele Commager, *A Pocket History of the United States* (New
York, NY, 1981). For a more critical history, see Howard Zinn, *A People's History of
the United States* (New York, NY, 1980). Educational histories that include descriptions
of social life include Lawrence Cremin, *American Education: The National Experience
1783–1976* (New York, 1980); Wayne J. Urban and Jennings L. Wagoner Jr., *American
Education: A History*, 3rd ed. (Boston, MA, 2004); and Joel Spring, *The American School
1642–2000*, 5th ed. (Boston, MA, 2001).

3. Again, a rich collection of sources exists for histories of childhood in the United
States. Of particular value is the wonderfully detailed Steven Mintz, *Huck's Raft: A
History of American Childhood* (Cambridge, MA, 2004), pages 7–118 are especially
relevant to the early nineteenth century. Other reliable sources for this era include

Joseph E. Illick, *American Childhoods* (Philadelphia, PA, 2002); Geraldine Youcha, *Minding the Children: Child Care in America from Colonial Times to the Present* (Cambridge, MA, 1995); and Jacqueline S. Reinier, *From Virtue to Character: American Childhood, 1775–1850* (New York, NY, 1996).

4. Stanley William Rothstein, *Schooling the Poor: A Social Inquiry into the American Educational Experience* (Westport, CT, 1994); David Ward, *Poverty, Ethnicity, and the American City, 1840–1935: Changing Conceptions of the Slum and the Ghetto* (Cambridge, UK, 1989); David Nasaw, *Children of the City: At Work and at Play* (New York, NY, 1985). For a general list of histories of urban development in the United States, see Lenwood G. Davis, ed., *A History of Urban Growth and Development: A Selected Bibliography of Published Works on the History of Urban Growth and Development in the United States, 1872–1972* (Monticello, IL, 1972).

5. Priscilla Ferguson Clement, *Growing Pains: Children in the Industrial Age, 1850–1890* (New York, NY, 1997); Michael B. Katz, *The Irony of Early School Reform: Educational Innovation in Mid-Nineteenth Century Massachusetts* (Boston, MA, 1968); Marvin Lazerson, *Origins of the Urban School: Public Education in Massachusetts, 1870–1915* (Cambridge, MA, 1971); Sol Cohen, "The Industrial Education Movement, 1906–1917," *American Quarterly* 20(1) (1968): 95–110. For more general histories, see David R. Meyer, *The Roots of American Industrialization* (Baltimore, MD, 2003); Walter Licht, *Industrializing America: The Nineteenth Century* (Baltimore, MD, 1995); Robert L. Heilbroner, *The Economic Transformation of America: 1600 to the Present* (Fort Worth, TX, 1994); and Julie Husband, *Daily Life in the Industrial United States, 1870–1900* (Westport, CT, 2004).

6. Selma Berrol, *Growing Up American: Immigrant Children in America, Then and Now* (New York, NY, 1995); Bernard J. Weiss, ed., *American Education and the European Immigrant, 1840–1940* (Urbana, IL, 1982); Oscar Handlin, *The Uprooted* (Boston, MA, 1990); Oscar Handlin, *Boston's Immigrants: A Study in Acculturation* (Cambridge, MA, 1979); John Higham, *Strangers in the Land: Patterns of American Nativism* (New Brunswick, NJ, 1955). For a remarkable first-person account of immigration, see Mary Antin, *The Promised Land* (Boston, MA, 1912).

7. Illick, *passim*; LeRoy Ashby, *Saving the Waifs: Reformers and Dependent Children, 1890–1917* (Philadelphia, PA, 1984); LeRoy Ashby, *Endangered Children: Dependency, Neglect, and Abuse in American History* (New York, NY, 1997); David MacLeod, *The Age of the Child: Children in America, 1890–1920* (New York, NY, 1998). See also Mintz, *passim*; Nasaw, *passim*; and Ward, *passim*.

8. In addition to the many sources cited in the previous section, see Steven Mintz, *Moralists and Modernizers: America's Pre-Civil War Reformers* (Baltimore, MD, 1995); Bruce Laurie, *Beyond Garrison: Antislavery and Social Reform* (Cambridge, UK, 2005); Louis Filler, *Abolition and Social Justice in the Era of Reform* (New York, NY, 1972). For a primary source representing one intellectual context for nineteenth-century reform, see Ralph Waldo Emerson, *The Political Emerson: Essential Writings on Politics and Social Reform* (Boston, MA, 2004).

9. General histories of the Progressive movement include Maureen A. Flanagan, *Progressives and Progressivisms: 1890s–1920s* (New York, NY, 2007); Michael E. McGerr, *A Fierce Discontent: The Rise and Fall of the Progressive Movement in America, 1870–1920* (Oxford, UK, 2005); and Elizabeth Sanders, *Roots of Reform: Farmers, Workers, and the American State, 1877–1917* (Chicago, IL, 1999). Sources focusing more on Progressive

education include Lawrence A. Cremin, *The Transformation of the School: Progressivism in American Education 1876–1957* (New York, NY, 1964); William J. Reese, *Power and the Promise of School Reform: Grassroots Movements during the Progressive Era* (New York, NY, 2002); and Herbert M. Kliebard, *The Struggle for the American Curriculum, 1893–1958*, 3rd ed. (New York, NY, 2004). Several relevant articles appear in Barbara Beatty, Emily D. Cahan, and Julia Grant, eds., *When Science Encounters the Child: Education, Parenting, and Child Welfare in 20th-Century America* (New York, NY, 2006).

    10. For a highly detailed, comparative account of child labor legislation during the nineteenth century, see Elizabeth Lewis Otey, *Report on Condition of Woman and Child Wage-Earners in the United States*, vol. 6, *The Beginnings of Child Labor Legislation in Certain States; a Comparative Study* (Washington, DC, 1910). See also Hugh D. Hindman, *Child Labor: An American History* (Armonk, NY, 2002).

    11. Michael S. Katz, *A History of Compulsory Education Laws* (Bloomington, IN, 1976); John W. Perrin, *The History of Compulsory Education in New England* (Meadville, PA, 1896); Paul Monroe, *Founding of the American Public School System*, vol. 1 (New York, NY, 1940); and especially Carl F. Kaestle, *Pillars of the Republic: Common Schools and American Society, 1780–1860* (New York, NY, 1983).

    12. There are now several competent general histories of special education and other sources examining these developments. These include Margret Winzer, *The History of Special Education: From Isolation to Integration* (Washington, DC, 1993); R. C. Scheerenberger, *A History of Mental Retardation* (Baltimore, MD, 1983); John Vickery Van Cleve and Barry Crouch, *A Place of Their Own: Creating the Deaf Community in America* (Washington, DC, 1989); Albert Deutsch, *The Mentally Ill in America: A History of Their Care and Treatment from Colonial Times* (New York, NY, 1949); Leo Kanner, *A History of the Care and Study of the Mentally Retarded* (Springfield, IL, 1964); Philip L. Safford and Elizabeth J. Safford, *A History of Childhood and Disability* (New York, NY, 1996). On Laura Bridgman see Maude Howe Elliott, *Laura Bridgman: Dr. Howe's Famous Pupil and What He Taught Her* (Boston, MA, 1903); Laura Elizabeth Howe Richards, *Laura Bridgman; The Story of an Opened Door* (New York, NY, 1928); Ernest Freeberg, *The Education of Laura Bridgman: First Deaf and Blind Person to Learn Language* (Cambridge, MA, 2001); and Elisabeth Gitter, *The Imprisoned Guest: Samuel Howe and Laura Bridgman, the Original Deaf-Blind Girl* (New York, NY, 2001). See also Robert L. Osgood, *The History of Inclusion in the United States* (Washington, DC, 2005), 17–22.

    13. James W. Trent Jr., *Inventing the Feeble Mind: A History of Mental Retardation in the United States* (Berkeley, CA, 1994), 60–95; Scheerenberger, *A History of Mental Retardation*, 109–36; Steven Gelb, "'Not Simply Bad and Incorrigible': Science, Morality, and Intellectual Deficiency," *History of Education Quarterly* 29 (Fall 1989): 359–79; Robert L. Osgood, *For "Children Who Vary from the Normal Type": Special Education in Boston 1838–1930* (Washington, DC, 2000), 43–52.

    14. Samuel Gridley Howe, quoted in Stanley Powell Davis, *Social Control of the Mentally Deficient* (New York, NY, 1930), 40, and in Anna M. Wallace, *History of the Walter E. Fernald State School* (n.d.: unpublished manuscript in author's possession), 10.

    15. Stewart E. Fraser and William W. Brickman, eds., *A History of International and Comparative Education: Nineteenth-Century Documents* (Glenview, IL, 1968), 21–180; Gerald L. Gutek, *A History of the Western Educational Experience* (Prospect Heights, IL, 1972); Robert Ulich, *Education in Western Culture* (New York, NY, 1965); Trent, *Inventing the Feeble Mind*, 46–52.

16. Cremin, *Transformation of the School*, 100–5; Kliebard, *The Struggle for the American Curriculum*, 36–44; S. Alexander Rippa, *Education in a Free Society*, 4th ed. (New York, NY, 1980), 221–24.

17. Osgood, For *"Children Who Vary,"* 21–30; Stanley K. Schultz, *The Culture Factory: Boston Public Schools, 1789–1860* (New York, NY, 1973); Joseph M. Wightman, comp., *Annals of the Boston Primary School Committee, from Its First Establishment in 1818, to Its Dissolution in 1855* (Boston, MA, 1860).

18. Osgood, For *"Children Who Vary,"* 30–41; Michael B. Katz, *Class, Bureaucracy, and Schools: The Illusion of Educational Change in America* (New York, NY, 1975).

19. Robert L. Osgood, "Undermining the Common School Ideal: Intermediate Schools and Ungraded Classes in Boston, 1838–1900," *History of Education Quarterly* 37 (Winter 1997): 375–98.

20. Osgood, For *"Children Who Vary,"* 93–166.

21. J. E. Wallace Wallin, *The Education of Handicapped Children* (Boston, MA, 1924), 31–43; Scheerenberger, *History of Mental Retardation*, 166–72; Winzer, *History of Special Education* 334–36; Joseph L. Tropea, "Bureaucratic Order and Special Children: Urban Schools, 1890s–1940s," *History of Education Quarterly* 27 (Spring 1987): 29–53; Barry M. Franklin, "Progressivism and Curriculum Differentiation: Special Classes in the Atlanta Public Schools, 1898–1923," *History of Education Quarterly* 29 (Winter 1989): 571–93; Marvin Lazerson, "The Origins of Special Education," in *Special Education Policies: Their History, Implementation, and Finance*, ed. Jay G. Chambers and William T. Hartman (Philadelphia, PA, 1983).

22. Kaestle, *passim*; Urban and Wagoner, *American Education*, 61–193; Spring, *American School*, 133–166.

23. Trent, *Inventing the Feeble Mind*, 60–130; Wallin, *Education of Handicapped Children*, 22–31; Winzer, *History of Special Education*, 82–120, 315–16. For a broader discussion of institutions in American life, see David J. Rothman, *The Discovery of the Asylum: Social Order and Disorder in the New Republic* (Boston, MA, 1971); David J. Rothman, *Conscience and Convenience: The Asylum and Its Alternatives in Progressive America* (Boston, MA, 1980); and Gerald Grob, *Mental Illness and American Society, 1875–1940* (Princeton, NJ, 1983).

24. Harriet McIntyre Foster, *The Education of Idiots and Imbeciles. A Paper Read Before the Social Science Association of Indiana* (Indianapolis, IN, 1879), 11.

25. Ibid., 3, 11–12.

26. Ida L. Gregory, "The Child's New America," *Journal of Education* 102 (July 2, 1925), 11; Joseph V. S. McClancy, "Preserving the Family," *Journal of the National Education Association* 1 (1916), 848–49.

27. R. L. Dugdale, *The Jukes: A Study in Crime, Pauperism, Disease and Heredity* (New York, NY, 1877); Henry Herbert Goddard, *The Kallikak Family: A Study in the Heredity of Feeblemindedness* (New York, NY, 1912); Douglas Baynton, *Forbidden Signs: American Culture and the Campaign against Sign Language* (Chicago, IL, 1996).

28. See, e.g., Amos W. Butler, "Some Families as Factors in Anti-Social Conditions," *Eugenics, Genetics and the Family* 1 (1923): 387–90; C. M. Louttit and Gladys D. Frith, "The Dorbets—A Feebleminded Family," *The Journal of Abnormal and Social Psychology* 29 (October–December 1934): 301–13; Robert L. Osgood, "The Menace of the Feebleminded: George Bliss, Amos Butler, and the Indiana Committee on Mental Defectives," *Indiana Magazine of History* 97 (December 2001): 253–77.

29. Mrs. Albion Fellows Bacon, "The Mental Defective in the Home," *Indiana Bulletin* 107 (December 1916): 384–85.

30. Jane Addams, "The Home and the Special Child," *Addresses and Proceedings of the National Education Association* (1908): 1127; Henry W. Thurston, "The Social Worker," *Journal of the National Education Association* 1 (1916): 850–51.

31. Ida M. Sutherland, "Divergent Views," *Exceptional Children* 4 (October 1937): 20–21.

2

Life in Institutions to 1940

Between 1800 and 1930 the worlds of children in the United States consisted of a nearly limitless array of environments, experiences, and expectations. From home to workplace, school to family, farm to small town to large city, American children experienced widely diverse lives and roles depending on age, ethnic background, geographic location, and family status. The condition of disability further divided the experiences of many children. The presence of an obvious and serious cognitive, physical, and/or behavioral impairment in a child often had far-reaching consequences for a child's life path. Large and small institutions, schools, homes, and other settings accommodated these children and largely defined who they were and what they could do. This chapter takes a much closer look at what children experienced on a daily basis in the larger public and private institutions from early in this nation's history until the 1930s.

BACKGROUND

During this period, public and private institutions for the disabled served chiefly persons affected by three essential categories of disability: deafness, blindness, and cognitive disability. At this time, cognitive disability was labeled "mental defect," "mental deficiency," or "feeblemindedness." Some of these institutions served children who exhibited two or more of these conditions. Officials placed such youngsters depending on the availability of space and the most prominent category of disability for the individual; for example, children who were totally deaf but also had relatively mild cognitive disability would most likely reside in an institution for the deaf. Some children whose disability led to more outlandish or disturbing modes of behavior ended up in institutions serving persons with profound mental illness, typically called asylums for the insane. Although they served a very minor portion of the population and were limited in number across the country, institutions for the deaf, the blind, and the mentally disabled wielded a powerful influence on public conceptions of disability and provided distinctive and ultimately controversial settings for the daily lives of disabled children.[1]

As historian David Rothman has insightfully pointed out, the development of institutions for dependent populations was not a foregone outcome or a to-be-expected feature of nineteenth-century reform movements. Rather, Rothman has argued that institutions for the disabled, poor, criminal, insane, miscreant youth, or other dependents arose because they "represented an effort to insure the cohesion of the community in new and changing circumstances." In the early nineteenth century, vast and dramatic changes seemed to overwhelm the public's sense of security and stability. In response, civic and philanthropic leaders established and sustained public and private institutions to "restore a necessary social balance to the new republic." While by no means certain such actions would prove successful, their hope was that "the asylum was to fulfill a dual purpose. . . . It would rehabilitate inmates and . . . set an example of right action for the larger society." For their founders, institutionalizing dependent populations represented a strong, upright approach to restoring social stability. Their goal was to "insure the safety of the republic and promote its glory."[2]

The mission statements or founding proclamations for individual institutions reveal much of the belief system on which they operated. All asserted the need for providing some sort of individual attention to persons whom society had condemned, ignored, or otherwise marginalized. The American School for the Deaf, founded as the Connecticut Asylum For the Education and Instruction of Deaf and Dumb Persons in 1817, stressed the importance of saving the souls of deaf persons "rescued from intellectual darkness" and "brought to the knowledge of the truth as it is in Jesus." Founders of institutions for the blind in the 1830s through the 1860s also frequently referenced the "darkness" or "gloom" "or "shadows and silence" faced by the blind and the need for education to address their "life of idleness and miserable dependence." Reports of European successes in educating deaf persons and blind persons inspired many Americans to support efforts to accomplish similar successes here, to "rescue" such persons from a life of solitude and provide them with the spiritual and practical means to participate more fully in society. Ironically, segregated institutions were seen from the outset as optimal places to realize these goals.[3]

Similar sensibilities contributed to the establishment of institutions for "idiots" or "the feeble-minded" (these were widely accepted clinical terms for this population at the time). As with other institutions of the era, "education" was entwined with considerations related to custodial care and protective isolation. Institutions in South Boston and in Barre, Massachusetts; Albany, New York; Media, Pennsylvania; and other states such as Ohio, Connecticut, Illinois, and Kentucky opened during the 1840s and 1850s as a means to provide more effective treatment of feebleminded children and adults. Social reformers such as Samuel Gridley Howe, Dorothea Dix, James B. Richards, and Charles Sumner as well as medical doctors such as Isaac Kerlin and Hervey B. Wilbur sought to develop residential settings to place and instruct "idiots." Many were inspired by similar efforts in England and France. Many public officials now recognized that mentally disabled persons were placed in settings such as workhouses, almshouses, jails, and "lunatic asylums" that were not appropriate locations for their education and treatment. The educational purpose of these new asylums for the mentally disabled is reflected in Howe's proclamation that the Massachusetts institution in South Boston was part of the "great chain" of common schools, and in Wilbur's assertions that "at the basis of all our efforts lies the principle that the human attributes of the intelligence, sensitivity, and will are not absolutely wanting in an idiot, but dormant and underdeveloped." Even so, historian James Trent Jr. argues, the superintendents of most of these facilities, who believed that such disabled individuals needed to be segregated in order to relieve families and society of their "burden," "were already planning for custodial facilities, not for an 'era of hope.' "[4]

Once institutions for the disabled became available, they grew steadily in size and number. By the end of the century, most states supported such facilities with some public funds, recognizing them as a necessary investment and as a governmental responsibility. The mechanisms by which individuals were placed in these institutions varied widely, however, depending to a large extent on the preferences of superintendents or stipulations made by legislatures. When Indiana opened its Asylum for Feebleminded Children as part of its

Soldier's and Sailor's Orphan's Home in Knightstown in 1879, there existed a great deal of uncertainty as to just who should be admitted, and how.

The act that founded the Indiana institution stated that "the purposes of this institution shall be to care for, support, train and instruct feeble minded children." However, the original resident applications suggest that relief of family and community frustration was as much a goal of sending a child there as instruction. Indeed, often a child's alleged "feeblemindedness" could not be claimed with any certainty, yet there seemed no other place that would be able to help her or him. A number of examples from the records of the Fort Wayne School for Feeble-minded Youth illustrate this point. Eighteen-year-old George G. Garard of Indianapolis "was sent here because his mother who is an invalid widdow [*sic*] could not keep him at home from which he would wander." Ellen Vale, a twelve-year old who lived in the Henry County Asylum, had a "rather long and flat" head and was a bedwetter. Her family physician reported that she "walks well and talks very well" but nonetheless stated that "I know her as a feeble-minded child." And Alice Scidmore, thirteen and from LaGrange County, first manifested her "peculiarity" at "three months by her perfect helplessness and obstinate costiveness" (that is, disagreeable behavior). Moreover, "she began to take steps at the age of three years," to talk at four, and "as a young child would [amuse herself] in all the mischief she can find." Nine-year-old John Wertenberger, who resided in the Wabash County Poor Farm, and merely "seemed to enjoy being alone" and "lisp[ed]," was admitted but discharged four months later "to live with his mother." While these examples are specific to Indiana, they accurately capture the state of lay public understanding of mental disability at the time.[5]

LIFE WITHIN THE INSTITUTIONS

In the early years of these institutions for mentally disabled children, formal instruction was the centerpiece of their daily lives and the primary expressed purpose of the institutions themselves. Most of these instructional programs were based on the "physiological method" of instruction developed by Edouard Seguin, a French teacher who emigrated to the United States around 1850. Seguin's method received great publicity in the United States during the 1850s and was touted as the most viable approach to the successful education of the severely mentally disabled. As Dr. Walter Fernald, superintendent of the Massachusetts institution in Waverly at the turn of the century explained,

Seguin's method involved a "physiological education of defective brains." Essentially, the method involved direct training of the five senses; focused development of the child's daily functions such as dressing, bathing, toileting, and eating; and constant effort to improve a child's basic motor skills and physical coordination. The institutions also typically featured fairly rigid daily schedules that involved not only formal instruction but also activities related to physical labor, personal hygiene, and social interaction.[6]

Because the superintendents of these institutions communicated regularly and grounded their facilities' programs in similar theoretical and instructional approaches, daily life in these institutions varied only slightly, at least in the first two decades of their operation. In 1880, Seguin himself reported on his series of visits to institutions in Massachusetts, New York, Pennsylvania, and Ohio. The institution at Barre in Massachusetts, he noted, consisted of several smaller buildings called cottages or homes for typical pupils while "those more seriously crippled, and those momentarily sick" resided in the main building under closer and more personal supervision. In this setting, thirty-six children were "educated more or less individually" by fifty teachers and assistants, most of whom were women. In Syracuse, New York, the institution employed a group "rotation" approach, where 150 students worked with only seven teachers on "more than forty different exercises." The groups shifted activities every thirty minutes over the course of the day; "this is movement for the inactive, objects for the aimless, and regularity for the unruly."[7]

In his visits to the Pennsylvania and Ohio facilities, Seguin noticed and described more specific manifestations of his physiological approach. In one he observed "about sixty children . . . execute movements timed by the piano or by their own songs. . . . To a person not familiar with the swiftness of the influence of example . . . it is perfectly incomprehensible how these idiots, a moment ago limp in their postures and movements, now assume attitudes and develop poses, some of which artists would not disdain." He also depicted in great detail how both programs used a child's hand as a focal point for instruction, employing stimulation, repetition, and imitation to develop the hand's motor skills. Seguin praised the artwork and other handicrafts produced during such lessons, which numbered over forty discrete exercises. "I would suggest . . . frequent hand exercises, in which the powers of perception, volition, and execution would be drilled to their utmost rapidity and precision," he advised. Noting that idiots "are human beings, that is, individuals capable of being sympathetically connected with their kind," Seguin stated that such group and "general training" was "the key to their education." He went on to describe other similar activities in playing with toys, listening and moving to music, and painting with bright colors.[8]

Seguin also addressed whether "joy" should be a factor in the education of "idiot" children. Describing the effects of a Christmas-tree lighting ceremony at Syracuse, where a heavily decorated tree was "set ablaze," he proclaimed, "At this sight hardly one face out of fifty looks idiotic. . . . What a lesson for the eye and for the heart!" At the school in Germantown, Pennsylvania, he told of a twelve-year-old child who stood on a table and told stories and fables, much to the delight of "the family of idiots" who were watching. Seguin noted that "the occupation of instructing idiots by making them happy has sometimes been condemned as in bad taste." However, he was delighted that "this Puritanism is gradually subsiding. . . . PLEASURE begins to be recognized as one of the stimuli in activity and morality." He also commented on the special powers of female teachers who, he believed, as did the common school reformers, had the patience and nurturing ability necessary to create a pleasurable approach to teaching. Seguin concluded that "the agitation for the improvement of idiots must not cease till we have provided for all of them."[9]

Most of these institutions followed fairly rigid daily schedules in the belief that routine and regimentation would contribute to more orderly behavior and more effective instruction. At the Indiana institution during the 1880s, children were divided into three "grades" depending on their assumed intellectual capabilities in order to improve "this unfortunate class, and [impart] to them such instruction as they can receive." One group focused on academic instruction; another more basic instruction; and the third emphasized physiological training and drill. Other daily activities included physical education and play as well as employment on the institution's farm or in the laundry and dining rooms. Usually the academic instruction took place in the morning, with work occurring in the afternoon. Most of the institutions also offered parties on various occasions in order to give the children some experience in social interaction. Children typically lived and slept in sex-segregated dormitories or wards, and in Indiana and elsewhere "they are not left alone at any time, either at work or play, and are protected and guarded in every particular."[10]

Life within Institutions: The Deaf

In institutions for the deaf, daily life followed similar patterns of instruction, work, and social activities, shaped by the particular needs and interests generated by their specific disability. Institutions for the deaf flourished by the latter part of the nineteenth century and featured a unique and vitally important division in their approach to instruction and student experience: they used either the manual (sign-language only) or the oral approach to communication. By 1940 only four states, due to their small size, did not sponsor such institutions; these states had formal contracts with other states to provide residential instruction. New York had seven institutions for the deaf, and several other states supported more than one. Fourteen institutions nationwide received funding from both public and private sources. Other models included residential facilities serving both deaf and blind children and adults in different departments, a practice started when resources were limited and then continued out of convenience. Children who were both deaf and blind usually resided in institutions for the deaf. Children who were both deaf and "feebleminded" typically were housed in institutions for the latter. In 1932 the White House Conference Committee on the Handicapped estimated between 1 and 2 million children in the United States were seriously hearing impaired.[11]

Like the American School for the Deaf at Hartford—the nation's first such facility—initially residential schools for the deaf used only a manual approach to teaching and communication and avoided any attempt to use voice or even lipreading. Administrators and teachers often came from the ranks of former students in deaf institutions. Daily programs were, like those in institutions for the mentally disabled, highly regimented and routinized. They began with breakfast, followed by academic classes in the morning and then by lunch and rest. In the afternoon there was vocational education followed by dinner, prayers, and one or two hours' free time before bed. Administrators used this approach to provide structure and teach the students habits of order and cooperation. Ultimately, "residential schools nourished the foundations of the American deaf community. Their academic and vocational instruction produced a core of educated deaf adults who shared a common language and similar experiences," as well as a powerful commitment to manualism and to the sanctity of the deaf community.[12]

By the late 1860s, however, a new approach began to be used in some of the established and in many of the newer institutions. Known as oralism, this approach treated deafness as "a handicap to be overcome and held that skill in speech and lipreading allowed deaf persons full access to normal society." The manualism–oralism debate dominated discourse among the deaf and those interested in their education for decades (and continues to this day). Supporters of oralism disdained the segregation, even isolation, from society that, they alleged, a strictly manual approach imposed on deaf persons. The first institution to use oral methods exclusively was the Clarke Institution for Deaf Mutes in Massachusetts, which opened in 1867.[13]

Oralism quickly began to challenge manualism as the preferred method of instruction and communication in institutions for the deaf. Differences between the two involved more than instruction. Manualism represented a mode of communication that symbolized the strength and integrity of a deaf culture and community. In contrast, the entire approach under oralism, according to historian Margret Winzer, "brought a new dogma to the education of deaf children." Oralism represented an approach that challenged positive notions of deafness and sought to extinguish isolated deaf communities; oralism was seen as the best mechanism to realize more through complete participation in normal society. Classroom instruction emphasized speech and lipreading skills, and the institution itself was set up to "[resemble] that of a large, well-regulated private family." By the early 1900s almost half of the deaf children in the country lived in oralist-practicing residential institutions or studied in day schools for the deaf. With the ascension of oralism, parents of deaf children had two fundamentally distinct approaches to choose from in determining how to educate children. The choice of an approach said as much about a family's attitude toward deafness as it did about educational practices.[14]

Life within Institutions: The Blind

Meanwhile, residential institutions for the blind implemented programs and regimens that were specifically tailored to address the consequences of blindness. As with institutions for the deaf, most states supported residential facilities for blind persons, while a few contracted such services out to other states. Also, many of the institutions received support from both public and private sources, and institutions for the blind typically served deaf–blind children. Again, children who were blind and feebleminded rarely attended institutions for the blind because their academic programs could not or would not accommodate significant mental disability. As of 1932, the White House Conference Committee on the Handicapped reported sixty-one residential schools for the blind serving more than 5,000 pupils. Northern states typically integrated their residential institutions by race, whereas southern states did not.[15]

Combining activities in academic instruction, vocational instruction, and specific sense training designed to compensate for the lack of sight, these institutions nonetheless sought to model a blind child's education as closely as possible on that for a sighted child. Programs aiming to alleviate the "hopeless darkness, wretchedness, and misery" that so many assumed was the lot of the blind emphasized a variety of stimulating methodologies. Physical training, including "physical culture and gymnasium work, together with recreation in outdoor play and sports," was a hallmark of education for the blind well into the 1900s. Also emphasized was musical instruction, "both vocal and instrumental," reflecting a durable but questionable public perception that blind children were especially adept at music. Students also learned to make various tools and engaged in a multitude of vocationally related manual work. As in all institutions for the disabled, students performed significant maintenance work for the institution: washing clothes, cleaning, cooking, and landscaping were typical daily activities for a child. "Domestic science" assumed special importance for girls. Academic instruction utilized raised texts, especially the New York point and Braille systems, and emphasized "oral teaching, communication, [and] religious instruction." As with the deaf, these institutions assumed a staunchly parental role in the lives of children, keeping them in a planned and predictable daily routine in order to strengthen their moral and social development.[16]

TURN-OF-THE-CENTURY DEVELOPMENTS: INSTITUTIONS FOR THE FEEBLEMINDED

By the early 1890s superintendents of the institutions for the mentally disabled had come to some important conclusions. Decades of experience with the residents of their facilities had convinced most of them that emphasis on academic instruction and intentions to "graduate" many of these children back into society were both misplaced. Instead, institutional life for these children became more custodial. Administrators reserved "school work" for only the most capable of the children. Most youngsters spent their time maintaining the institution's physical plant and working to generate income or save money for the institution. With the advent of more negative views of the capabilities and worth of "feeble-minded" individuals, new mechanisms for organizing and controlling their lives took hold.

The state of Indiana again represented an instructive example of how these developments occurred. By 1890, the Indiana Institution for The Mentally Disabled had relocated to Fort Wayne and assumed a new name: The Indiana School for Feebleminded Youth. In 1886, the Asylum proclaimed that it "employed, by skillful teachers, the most approved modern methods of awakening and strengthening the intellectual faculties of this unfortunate class." Over the next several years, however, this academic focus shrank noticeably—and permanently. The institution's head physician reported in 1893 that while "it seems to be confidently expected upon the part of not a few parents whose children are committed . . . that the latter will speedily become transformed into almost perfect beings, mentally, morally and physically," he had to acknowledge that such an achievement would be "as difficult as it is for the leopard to change his spots or the Ethiopian his skin." Over the next several decades, officials became increasingly resigned to the primarily custodial and protective role of the institution.[17]

In the early 1890s its new superintendent, Alexander Johnson, began his practice of issuing annual reports that included factual information as well as theoretical speculation on feeblemindedness and those who were institutionalized because of it. The 1894 annual report classified the residents of the institution into several "grades." First were those "slightly feeble in mind [yet] still so backward that they can not receive an education in the public schools of the State." A second included children "with minds so feeble and wills so wanting that they can never become self-controlling citizens . . . yet [they are] susceptible of a great deal of education." These constituted about half the resident population. A third class, the "educable custodials," "can receive little of ordinary school instruction, but . . . are yet capable of much physical training." The fourth and last class, was "the lowest grade of idiots or imbeciles, whose lives are almost wholly vegetative. For them the school proper can do nothing." Johnson saw his institution as primarily a "school" for the upper two grades and an "asylum" for the lower two. At the time of this report, Johnson noted the lowest "class" represented about 12 percent of the current population but about 60 percent of applicants for admission on the waiting list.[18]

These annual reports also began to offer more intimate glimpses of individual children—most likely in an effort to convey to the public the severe nature of disability found among the residents as well as the value of being institutionalized. For example when one boy, "J.H.," arrived, "he was extremely nervous, of a quarrelsome disposition, could not stand straight, and would not remain in a seat even a few moments at a time. He is now quiet, and though fond of play, does not quarrel with his companions. When he stands he is like a little soldier. . . . This child hears, but does not speak, and on account of the peculiar formation of his mouth will probably never be able to do so." Another child, "F.A.," also supposed to have been mute, speaks only in a whisper, but has learned many words. His extreme bashfulness probably hinders him to a great extent." The report also noted the case of "W.F.," a twelve-year-old boy who, claimed the principal of the school, would feign epileptic seizures "when convenient. . . . He always waited until the teacher or attendant could give undivided attention to him." As a "treatment," the boy "was deprived of any play at which he might be hurt should he have a convulsion. . . . He was allowed to do hardly anything, because he was a 'spasm boy.' In vain did he protest that he did not have spasms. This treatment was continued for about three months, and he is now, I believe, effectively cured." To underscore the value of institutionalization, the principal also reported on two children who had severe cases of stuttering, with one of them having "spells of screaming and stammering, and would bite his hands." Both allegedly made great strides at the institution, went home on vacation, then returned "almost as bad as [they] had ever been."[19]

By the mid-1890s the daily schedules at the institution had become highly stratified and regimented according to the "grade" of the child. Kindergarten work occupied children in the custodial classes and was allegedly used "with marked success." Even so, the abilities of these children were quite limited: "They can learn but little besides caring for themselves, lacing or buttoning shoes and clothing, playing, and the use of their hands and feet. . . . It is hard to imagine the necessity for teaching a child to play, but such is the case." The second ("educable") class was divided into seven different grades, and they engaged in various levels of kindergarten and academic work. Several of the students studied piano or participated in band or drum corps. The highest grades of children moved from academic into "industrial" work, which was "the pre-eminent central power of education to-day" for intellectual, physical, and moral development. During daylight hours, all children spent time outside in gardens or playing in the fresh air, and all who were capable participated in calisthenics, military drill, and physical exercises. Evening activities included more physical games, singing, board games, and occasional festivals and other forms of entertainment. The 1894 report noted that "the great moral rule, 'Get the heart right,' is the physical rule we would follow. If the heart and lungs can be kept in good condition the muscles are easily trained." A.C., for example, "was of a lethargic disposition, showing a disinclination to work, and was very backward at school. He was put at half-day work, and immediately showed signs of improvement. His mind needed the impulse of a live body—not a half dead one." This regimen of movement between academic and physical activity—with the "custodial" cases engaging in much more physical than mental activity—was commonplace throughout the United States in institutions for the mentally disabled.[20]

Within ten years, then, a noticeable shift had occurred from an emphasis on academic and intellectual development to one focused on physical training and the development of acceptable individual and collective behavior. By 1898, C. M. Lawrence, a visitor to the Indiana institution, noted the "graded" approach to organizing the children but barely mentioned any authentic academic work. Instead he divided his observations into "amusements," "music," "physical culture," "special senses," and "nature study." He enthusiastically described the games, parties, and holidays celebrated on a regular basis; the extensive activities in instrumental and vocal music; the calisthenics, sports, drills, and manual labor in the outdoors; the thirty children receiving training to improve their sense functions. Each of these aimed to improve the habits, instincts, and attitudes of the children—as well as make the work more efficient. "When the children have learned to love and help each other," he wrote, greater numbers can be kept together, and in this and other ways reduce the cost of their support per capita. In this lies the hope for the complete care of the feeble-minded."[21]

During the early years of the twentieth century, then, institutions for the mentally disabled nationwide shifted their efforts away from "improvement" or "education" to custodial care that would be cost-efficient, protective of society, and protective of the inmates. One important change was the aging of the inmate population: the ratio of children to adults steadily shifted away from children. This change occurred as adults who entered as children did not leave, and the already overcrowded institutions began admitting adults, especially women between the ages of fifteen and forty-five. The potential childbearing years represented a particular threat to experts who believed in the exclusively hereditary nature of mental defect. Thus, under the theory of eugenics, they advocated confinement and sterilization as the best means to prevent procreation of mentally retarded persons. With more adults and fewer children to care for, custodial care and work-related activities took precedence over academic endeavors. Furthermore, even for those youngsters who remained institutionalized, superintendents had convinced themselves that academic instruction was lost on children who simply could not learn or find value in it. Instead, school classes within institutions began to focus on "habit training," vocational training, and socialization along the lines practiced at the Indiana institution. Such approaches were loosely grounded in Seguin's physiological method but emphasized physical and moral more than intellectual development. Over time inmates assumed a large proportion of the work-related obligations necessary to maintain asylums, thereby reducing costs and easing the problem of staff turnover. By the early 1900s, academic instruction had become a minor aspect of daily life at best in institutions for the mentally disabled.[22]

A fundamental change in institutional life also occurred as many of the institutions adopted a colony or farm-plan approach to housing and daily activity. As with the initial development of institutions in the early nineteenth century, the introduction of the cottage or "community-like" approach to institutional design and programming occurred in all forms of institutions at the time—not just those for the disabled but those serving criminals, the mentally ill, dependent families, and miscreant youth. The concept emphasized a stronger focus on individual development as well as on reproducing a more "natural" daily existence similar to that found in local communities—common themes in Progressive reform. The "congregate" model, in which all inmates lived in one large building, lost favor over time. It was often replaced by a "cottage" model—similar to the one at the Clarke Institution—which grouped children into smaller collectives meant to emulate family life. Later some institutions adopted the farm colony plan, with separate facilities on working farms for male inmates in order to segregate them from females and generate income and food for the institution. Both cottages and farm colonies emphasized the perceived need to provide more "normal" living environments for inmates as well as to ensure efficient and cost-effective operation. The farm colony model predominated in institutions for the mentally disabled by 1910, ensuring that a life spent working outdoors became normal for a large number of boys and young men. Meanwhile, girls and women in the institutions lived in smaller groups and contributed heavily to the maintenance of the facility through "domestic science" such as cooking, cleaning, laundering, and other daily chores. The colony approach generally demonstrated greater success at returning inmates to open society in independent living situations or back with their families. Nevertheless, returnees still constituted only a minor percentage of those committed to institutional care.[23]

By the 1930s institutions for the mentally disabled had a long history. They were not fading away—most were overcrowded. Parents, other family members, advocates for the disabled, and concerned citizens expressed confusion about institutional purposes and accomplishments. But in 1923, as he reflected on the role of these institutions in American society, Alexander Johnson spoke for most of those involved in their operation when he said:

> There is much we do in social work with a certain questioning. The
> danger of doing for people what they ought to do for themselves is
> always present. . . . In all institutions, especially those for children,
> such dangers threaten. The term "institutionism" is recognized as
> denoting something to be feared and avoided.
>
> But in the work for the feeble-minded all this disappears. They
> are children now and always will be. The sooner they are institution-
> alized; that is the sooner they learn to yield to the kindly direction
> of those who care for them, the better. They should never go into
> the outside world as free citizens with all that implies.[24]

TWENTIETH-CENTURY DEVELOPMENTS: INSTITUTIONS
FOR THE DEAF AND FOR THE BLIND

On the other hand, institutions for the deaf and the blind were seen in a different, more benevolent light. They were seen as true schools and educational
institutions rather than custodial warehouses or pseudo-prisons. Although the
disabilities of deafness and blindness were viewed as catastrophic conditions,
the children were seen as more intelligent, more capable of learning, and far
more suited (at least for deaf children trained in oralism) to be mainstreamed
into regular society. The institutions themselves remained much more stable
in terms of what they offered and what they did.

By no means, however, were these institutions for the deaf and for the
blind free from critique or suspicion. In addition to the heated controversy
over manualism versus oralism in deaf education, the rise of day schools serving children who were deaf or blind (see Chapter 3) challenged assumptions
about the propriety and effectiveness of a residential approach to instruction
and socialization. For both populations, day school advocates argued that the
nonresidential approach allowed the children to experience a more natural life
in the family, home, and community and that, conversely, institutionalization
deprived children of that "healthy, normal life" where "the home . . . should
be the center of the affection and interests of every child." Some argued that
institutional life developed peculiar personalities and behaviors among its resident students. Supporters of the oralist approach to deaf education dominated
the control of and teaching in day schools for the deaf, and they argued that
keeping the children in the community and allowing them to attend public

school with their normal peers gave them the best chance for social acceptance and success. Also, day school instruction typically cost significantly less than residential school instruction.[25]

In contrast, supporters of the residential approach asserted that institutional instruction offered better opportunities for specialized instruction as well as a more secure and supportive environment for children whose disability drew unwanted attention and often derision. After experiencing years of criticism of institutions, Merle Frampton and Ellen Kerney, educators of the blind, prepared a fierce defense of the institutional approach to teaching blind children and a critique of the day-school movement. They stated that "the residential school for the blind has, from its inception up to the present, reflected the concrete expression of the people's will" and that nothing has "detracted from the magnificent contributions of the residential school to blind people." Supporters of residential institutions for the deaf also defended their approach for much the same reason. In particular, advocates of the manual approach viewed the residential institution as a bastion of protection for the deaf way of life, essential to its survival. Although carrying significantly higher status than the mentally disabled population, deaf and/or blind persons in residential institutions thus still found themselves in settings that engendered considerable doubt and controversy.[26]

Nonetheless, residential institutions—whether for the deaf, blind, or mentally disabled—represented only part of this history. As the day-school controversy suggests, public schools and communities also offered settings in which children with disabilities lived, learned, and grew. The next chapter will explore these other settings in greater detail.

NOTES

1. Differentiating between insanity and "feeblemindedness" during the 1800s was at best an inexact and uncertain science. One source describing the evolution of such attempts at differentiation is Steven A. Gelb, "'Not Simply Bad and Incorrigible': Science, Morality, and Intellectual Deficiency," *History of Education Quarterly* 29 (Fall 1989): 359–79. See also Albert Deutsch, *The Mentally Ill in America: A History of Their Care and Treatment from Colonial Times*, 2nd ed. (New York, 1949).

2. David J. Rothman, *The Discovery of the Asylum: Social Order and Disorder in the New Republic* (Boston, 1971), xviii–xix.

3. Cited in John Vickery Van Cleve and Barry Crouch, *A Place of Their Own: Creating the Deaf Community in America* (Washington, DC, 1989), 46; Harry Best, *Blindness and the Blind in the United States* (New York, 1934), 312–20.

4. Cited in James W. Trent Jr., *Inventing the Feeble Mind: A History of Mental Retardation in the United States* (Berkeley, CA, 1994), 17. See also pp. 2–3, 14–31. Walter E. Fernald, *Proceedings and Addresses of the National Education Association*, 1893, 207; R. C. Scheerenberger, *A History of Mental Retardation* (Baltimore, MD, 1983), 99–107; Margret Winzer, *The History of Special Education: From Isolation to Integration* (Washington, DC, 1993), 93–96, 112–15.

5. State of Indiana, *General Laws, 1879*, Chapter VIII, Sec. 2; Indiana State Archives, Commission on Public Records, Fort Wayne School for Feebleminded Youth, Inmate Packets 1–29, Box R1887–030671.

6. Fernald, *Proceedings and Addresses*, 204.

7. E. Seguin, *Report on Education*, 2nd ed., 1880, 101–3.

8. E. Seguin, *Report on Education*, 104–9.

9. E. Seguin, *Report on Education*, 109–11.

10. State of Indiana, *34th Report of the Superintendent of Public Instruction* (hereafter referred to as *ISPI*), 1885/1886, 129–30.

11. Harry Best, *Deafness and the Deaf in the United States: Considered Primarily in Relation to Those Sometimes More or Less Erroneously Known as "Deaf-Mutes"* (New York, 1943), 433–44; White House Conference on Child Health and Protection, *The Handicapped Child: Report of the Committee on Physically and Mentally Handicapped* (New York, 1933), 420.

12. Van Cleve and Crouch, *A Place of Their Own*, 47–54.

13. Winzer, *History of Special Education*, 126, 128–29.

14. Winzer, *History of Special Education*, 129.

15. Best, *Blindness and the Blind*, 334–41; White House Conference, *The Handicapped Child*, 58–66.

16. Best, *Blindness and the Blind*, 317, 384–87; Winzer, *History of Special Education*, 207–10.

17. *34th Report of ISPI*, 1885/1886, 129; *14th Annual Report of the Indiana School for Feebleminded Youth* (hereafter referred to as *ARISFMY*), 1892, 13. The trend to custodialism also occurred in other institutions in this era. See David J. Rothman, *Conscience and Convenience: The Asylum and Its Alternatives in Progressive America* (New York, 2002).

18. *15th ARISFMY*, 1893, 16–17.

19. *16th ARISFMY*, 1894, 25, 30–32.

20. *16th ARISFMY*, 1894, 25–30.

21. *20th ARISFMY*, 1898, 18–22.

22. Trent, *Inventing the Feeble Mind*, 99–112; Scheerenberger, *History of Mental Retardation*, 158–60; Winzer, *History of Special Education*, 217–19.

23. Rothman, *Conscience and Convenience*, 5–7; Scheerenberger, *History of Mental Retardation*, 160–63.

24. Alexander Johnson, *Adventures in Social Welfare: Being Reminiscences of Things, Thoughts, and Folks During Forty Years in Social Work* (Fort Wayne, IN, 1923), 177. On family perceptions see Trent, *Inventing the Feeble Mind*, 112–16.

25. Best, *Blindness and the Blind*, 342–43; Best, *Deafness and the Deaf in the United States*, 445–50; Philip L. Safford and Elizabeth J. Safford, *A History of Childhood and Disability* (New York, 1996), 144–48; Winzer, *History of Special Education*, 317–20.

26. Best, *Blindness and the Blind*, 343–44; Best, *Deafness and the Deaf*, 450–55; White House Conference, *The Handicapped Child*, 72–78; Safford and Safford, *History of*

Childhood and Disability, 146–50; Merle F. Frampton and Ellen Kerney, *The Residential School: Its History, Contributions, and Future* (New York, 1953), iii. *The Residential School* contains numerous statements taken from sources covering many decades that vociferously defend institutional life. For an excellent example of a celebratory institutional history that addresses the era under discussion, see Walter B. Hendrickson, *From Shelter to Self Reliance: A History of the Illinois Braille and Sight-Saving School* (Jacksonville, IL, 1972), 68–155.

3

Public Schools and the Accommodation of Students with Disabilities to 1940

As institutions for the disabled grew in both size and influence during the nineteenth and early twentieth centuries, the nation's public schools underwent their own remarkable transformation. In cities across America, large, stratified, and highly structured systems of public education developed, while in small towns and farm communities one-room schoolhouses proliferated. Publicly supported elementary and secondary education became a major public concern in the United States. At the same time, attitudes and beliefs regarding disability became more negative, and disabled children were broken down into ever more specialized categories. The number of children identified as disabled grew noticeably. It became the task of public schools to identify, segregate, instruct, and control children whose disabilities were seen as difficult, dangerous, or untreatable.

EARLY EXPERIENCES: UNDIFFERENTIATED SETTINGS

In 1838, when city officials in Boston established "Intermediate Schools," or "Schools for Special Instruction," they hoped to isolate temporarily older, non–English-speaking immigrant children. In these special schools, such children could learn to read and write in English and thus prepare to return to their regular classrooms. However, Boston soon found that other children who disrupted standard classroom practices and demanded too much of an overworked teacher's valuable time and attention could also profit from being removed to segregated classrooms and schools. Consequently, the Boston public school officials learned an important lesson that would not be lost on other city school systems: as public elementary and secondary schools grew in size and became more crowded, stratified, and regimented, it became necessary to provide alternative placements for children who were seriously struggling intellectually, physically, or behaviorally.

Before 1900, Boston was but one of many cities to establish such *undifferentiated* settings—that is, classes or schools that did not organize instruction according to age and that therefore included all ages of children with a wide range of capabilities. New Haven, Connecticut; Cleveland, Ohio; and New York City created settings for the "incorrigible," the "unruly," or "the most serious cases of imbecility" during the 1870s. For example, a class in Cleveland that opened around 1875 hoped to help all its students "become as normal children." Unfortunately it lasted only a year, after which time "all were aware that their experiment was doomed to failure...the class disbanded...[and] the poor teacher suffered a mental collapse which necessitated a sojourn at [the] State Hospital."[1] Such settings—with the notable exception of the Horace Mann School, Boston's day school for deaf children that opened in 1869—typically included children exhibiting all kinds of problematic mental, physical, and behavioral conditions. Boston's intermediate schools, Detroit's "truant school" (opened in 1883), the New York and Cleveland classes noted above, and classes in Philadelphia and Baltimore served students who "were linked by their threat to classroom order." These "repositories" contained children who were "intellectually backward, recalcitrant...incorrigibles, truants, and low achievers."[2] Designed to impose order on difficult children and ease pressures on a rigid curriculum and overcrowded regular classrooms, such settings became notorious. As one indication of this, Boston's intermediate schools and ungraded classes became known as the "Botany Bays" of that city's public school system by 1880 (Botany Bay was at the time a notorious penal colony in Australia).[3]

Regrettably, little direct or hard evidence exists that reveals what life in such undifferentiated settings was like for students and teachers, although labels such as "Botany Bay" and the nervous breakdown of one of the first Cleveland public school teachers to engage in such work certainly are suggestive. By the mid-1840s, intermediate school teachers in Boston requested extra pay because of the demanding nature of their jobs. They taught mostly immigrant children, who the superintendent John Philbrick described as "slovenly urchins...little better than semi-barbarians." Philbrick also noted that "the teachers in these schools have an arduous and difficult task to perform, and they need special encouragement and assistance." A city report in 1857 complained that "the very existence of such a class of schools, composed of children whose early education and moral instruction have been neglected, or who have not been favored by an ordinary share of intellectual endowments, naturally tends to abuses which no regulations, however stringent, can prevent." These statements strongly suggest that life in these classrooms proved extremely trying for teachers and students.[4]

Such concerns ultimately led to the intermediate schools' reorganization as "ungraded" (another term indicating undifferentiated) classes in Boston. However, their function as a dumping ground for students who could not succeed in regular classrooms continued. Despite repeated efforts to improve the lot of the ungraded classes, they continued to grow, without improving their reputation within the Boston school system. Teachers persisted in lobbying for more money and were repeatedly denied. All too often, teachers assigned to the classrooms were of poor quality and received virtually no special training. Students came from immigrant backgrounds; by the end of the century most were from southern or eastern Europe. These children struggled with severe language difficulties, radically different cultural expectations, and the growing public belief that immigrants were obstinate and intellectually wanting. In 1895, a school supervisor assigned to examine the ungraded classes claimed that their students were "troublesome and hindered the progress of others" and determined that "even the most capable teachers shrink from assuming a charge which makes such large demands upon their patience, strength, and skill."[5]

Boston's situation reflected similar practices around the country. One observer commented on the early efforts in New York to establish "ungraded" or "special" classes that "the work in New York for mentally deficient children is in a formative but chaotic state at the present time. The terms 'ungraded' and 'special' classes are used synonymously, and cover those for wayward, backward, and mentally deficient children. It is impossible to tell how many there are for the latter, for backward and mentally deficient children are often in class together." In Philadelphia, Baltimore, and Detroit, early efforts to establish similar segregated settings led to the inclusion of a wide range of students: "'irregular attendants, and neglected children,' 'unmanageable in the regular schools,' 'incorrigible, backward and otherwise defective pupils,' 'a type who could not be effectively taught in the regular classes,' and children of immigrants." In Boston as in these other cities, the vast majority of students were male. The widely diverse nature of the children's disabilities within such classes—referred to as "omnium gatherum" classes by one Boston superintendent—revealed both the uncertainty regarding identification and diagnosis as well as the pressures to maintain order in rigid, highly stratified school systems. Moreover, they suggest a wide range of experiences for both students and teachers, hallmarked by confusion, frustration, and resignation.[6]

THE RISE OF DIFFERENTIATED SETTINGS

After 1900, with increased experience and the use of more sophisticated methods of identifying specific kinds of disability, large urban schools eventually overcame the need for the undifferentiated, collective "dumping grounds" characteristic of the nineteenth century. As noted in Chapter 1, in the twentieth century, school systems in large cities across the country established complex structures for the segregated education of children with identified disabilities. In such settings, curricula and other programmed activities could be geared toward a specific condition or set of conditions. Fortunately, we have some record of what life in such school-based settings was like.

It should be noted, however, that before and even after establishing extensive special education structures some public school officials questioned whether children with obvious and significant disabilities belonged in public schools at all. Opinions varied widely on this subject. An unattributed statement in the February 1921 edition of the *Journal of Education* lamented the "neglect of sub-normal persons" but argued that such individuals should be treated in the residential institutions, as "no defectives under any conditions should be allowed in public schools, in country or city." Dr. George Bliss, superintendent of the Indiana School for Feebleminded Youth, wrote in 1920:

> We need a social conscience that will not tolerate feeble-minded children in the public schools, but will demand either their segregation in special classes, or their removal to a suitable institution for their education and care. Defective children in the public schools are not only a burden to a conscientious teacher, but as they develop into puberty may be a positive menace to the discipline and morals of any schoolroom.

James T. Byers, president of the national Committee on Provision for the Feeble-Minded, also complained about the presence of disabled children in the schools: "You teachers know them better than I. There are these children that do not get along, that are taking your time and your attention to an unlimited extent, taking it from the other children very largely. They are a drag upon the school, day after day and year after year; and the State is paying the expense of keeping them in the same class, duplicating the work, and still they don't make progress."[7]

Nonetheless, supporters of using the public schools to educate children with disabilities carried the day, as the growth of special education programs in urban public schools demonstrated. Enrollment in such programs grew during the early 1900s due to strengthened compulsory attendance laws nationwide and the realization that public schools were often the only placement option for disabled children. In his introduction to Meta Anderson's widely read 1917 book *Education of Defectives in Public Schools*, Henry Herbert Goddard noted that "whether these children should be kept in the public schools and there trained or be provided for by some other method. . . . The fact remains that in all probability these children will remain in the public schools for a long time to come, if for no other reason than the lack of adequate machinery to provide for them elsewhere." Others were more charitable about such children's presence in the schools. The superintendent of the Vineland School for the Feeble-Minded in New Jersey, E. R. Johnstone, stated frankly: "Public-school men may say, 'This is not our problem.' To say this means nothing. The children are here; they are present in the public school in large numbers. They cannot be turned out. . . . The only thing to do is to give them the best care and training possible." Johnstone also argued that the special classes could be used "as a laboratory for public school classes" to test new methods of instruction that would benefit all children. Other public school officials commented on the value of not only special classes for the mentally "defective" but also those serving children who were "crippled," blind, deaf, "incorrigible," or chronically ill.[8]

While public pronouncements suggested that the primary motivations for creating these programs were educational in nature—such settings would benefit the instruction of disabled children and, just as important, those of "normal" children—other factors contributed as well. Historians Joseph Tropea and Marvin Lazerson maintain that special education programs fulfilled the desire to control certain elements of the population and enhance the efficiency of school systems. In the minds of most officials, public schools—especially those in the large cities—needed to function as agents of social control and assimilation of diverse ethnic groups, and segregated settings aided such efforts considerably. By including children with identified disabilities within the public school system, those with low intellect—the "subnormals," "dullards," and "morons"—could be monitored more carefully and channeled into constructive or appropriate activities. Programs addressing physical, sensorial, or other obvious impairments could operate separately from the regular classrooms, thus streamlining their operation and that of the system as a whole. By 1920, most sizable cities had public school systems with a number of classes, schools, or other settings dedicated to children with a variety of specific disabilities.[9]

SPECIAL CLASSES FOR THE MENTALLY DISABLED: STUDENT SELECTION

The flagship settings for special education programs across the United States were classes for "feebleminded" or "mentally defective" children. The first such "special" class opened in Providence, Rhode Island, in 1896. Over the next four years, similarly designated classes began in Boston, New York, Chicago, Philadelphia, and other large cities. Officials labeled students in such classes as "backward," "subnormal," "stupid," or "mental defectives apparently above the 'purely imbecile' grade." A 1927 national survey of over 500 cities in the United States showed that there were about 4,000 such classes enrolling more than 78,000 children.[10]

When schools first formed these classes, the characteristics of the students and the nature of the activities they engaged in varied widely. Until the advent of large-scale, group mental testing between the late 1910s and the 1920s, identifying children appropriate for special class placement was mostly subjective and sometimes included a medical component. In Boston, for example, teachers and/or principals brought "eligible" children to the attention of Dr. Arthur Jelly, who from 1900 through the 1910s examined such children and determined their appropriateness for special class placement. In New York City one teacher, Elizabeth Farrell, was responsible for selecting the first "ungraded class in Public School No. 1 in Manhattan" in 1899. Farrell selected from "chronic truants" and other children "in the regular grades . . . [who] were getting little or no profit from their attendance." Many in this first class had little interest in school and considerably more interest in the various attractions of street life. They were the "odds and ends" that confounded teachers and school administrators. "There were over-age children, so-called naughty children, and the dull and stupid children. They were taken from any and every school grade.... [Their] mental habits were of the worst kind—little power of attention to abstract notions, will-power or a wishy-washy character or else so obstructed that action was frequently paralyzed." Almost twenty years later the method of referral by educators of mentally deficient children to special classes remained much the same. Typically, the principal reviewed "deficient cards" sent by teachers but also personally observed children who were clearly struggling in classrooms: "As I look at them I see the vacant stare, or the beseeching glance of questioning which says to the principal . . . Why can I not answer like the smart boys? . . . I should like to do things too. Why can't I do them? . . . All these questions well up in the eyes of this little child, so young and already so disappointed." Most cities used some combination of subjective referral followed by a medical examination until the late 1910s.[11]

The introduction and acceptance of standardized intelligence tests—first the individual test, then the group-administered test—dramatically affected the selection process for special classes for students with mental disabilities. First introduced in the United States in 1916, the Binet–Simon intelligence test—revised and issued by Dr. Lewis Terman as the Stanford–Binet test—provided hungry school districts and other interested parties with what they believed to be a truly objective, "scientific" approach to identifying mentally "defective" children. Although some doubted the wisdom of test administration for this purpose as well as the tests' reliability in identifying mental disability, most educators, medical doctors, psychologists, and other professionals in the field hailed the tests as an excellent addition to the identification process. By the early 1920s school districts, psychological "clinics," and other agencies administered literally hundreds of thousands of the tests annually. Evaluation typically relied heavily on test results but might also include a physical examination, a family history, an assessment of schoolwork, a personal "social history," and an evaluation of "moral reactions."[12]

SPECIAL CLASSES: LIFE IN THE CLASSROOM

Once a student had been identified and placed in a special class, she or he encountered a variety of conditions, instructional content and strategies, and assumptions regarding her or his capabilities as well as character. Although "special" classes supposedly only enrolled "mental defectives," many included students from various backgrounds with different capabilities. In 1922 an observer in one such class noted, for example:

> In another community of the same state the one special class was so evidently a "dumping ground" for all kinds of non-conforming pupils that the teacher in charge was quite ready to admit it. There were boys and girls of different ages and races, Jews, Italians, negroes [sic] and others, and of very different physical and mental caliber. Some did rather creditable work in writing, reading, number, art and manual pursuits, and the writer was told that the teacher had returned a handsome percentage to the regular grades. Others were distinctly psychopathic, or neglected, or deficient, or what not. The teacher's task was not one to be envied.[13]

Such a description was reminiscent of one made in 1903 by a Boston observer who noted that fifteen students in the city's first special class had various conditions including "rickets . . . convulsions . . . epilepsy . . . deformed palates, and only three had good teeth."[14] This description, made before specialized testing and placement of mentally disabled children in special classes, sounds suspiciously like the reality for many such children in a later and presumably more enlightened era.

For the most part, however, the advent of group intelligence testing and the development of settings for other specialized disabling conditions helped administrators assign students to classes with greater accuracy and precision. Massachusetts required teachers of its special classes to "First, study the individual and determine his ability. Second, make sure the task assigned is within his ability. Third, insist on successful completion of each task attempted." Other states and cities likewise aimed for efficient instruction in special classes. By 1922, in Detroit educators had organized "Special A" and "Special B" classes based on a student's age, ability, and assumed occupational capability after finishing his or her education. Cleveland and Boston both established special class clusters and centers that gathered special class students under one roof and permitted easier movement among settings depending on ability. By this time, officials typically placed a child in a particular special class based almost exclusively on his or her score on an intelligence test.[15]

In the early twentieth century, the activities within the special classes became more formalized, much like the regular school curriculum in structure and detail but distinctive in content and methodology. The earliest special class curriculum employed some of Seguin's ideas on "physiological education" but also incorporated elements of kindergarten methodology as well as of standard manual and vocational training. New York's Elizabeth Farrell identified two procedures for determining the most appropriate starting point for a new child in a special class. The first was "the negative procedure," which involved challenging a child to engage in intellectual and motor tasks normal for a child her or his age and working "backward" to the point where the child can actually accomplish a given task. The second consisted of "localization," where one "begins with the most elementary workings of the child's neuro-muscular system, and climbs upward by means of very short, definite, more complex workings until the arrest in development has been reached." Farrell then asserted that imitation was an essential element of any special class instruction as it was "the first step in mental development." Years of experience led special class teachers across the nation to develop more formal curricula. For example, between 1914 and 1928, the Boston Special Class Teachers Club published a series of editions of their special class curriculum, *The Boston Way*. This volume offered detailed suggestions for a wide range of content and methodologies considered appropriate in the special class setting.[16]

   Most early special class teachers followed similar procedures, working with individual children in a process of mutual trial, error, and discovery. Indeed, among the richest images of life in the special class are narratives describing individual teacher efforts with individual students. One of the most vivid comes from Harriet Lyman, the teacher in Boston's second special class:

> The children can be graded together in very few subjects, and show a great diversity in their various small attainments. One can read readily, but cares nothing for a book, has little language of his own, and no idea of number. Others, who have been years under instruction, can copy a little writing, but cannot read a word. Some are fond of drawing, but the present class all are extremely deficient in the simplest number work, relying upon memory without any exercise of reason. Some are garrulous, others strangely silent as if from years of repression. One is heavy and inert, another never motionless.[17]

In 1917, an especially sanguine view of special class work came from Quincy, Illinois, where teacher Anna Kordsiemon praised the value of "construction work" as an effective approach to stimulate and improve both mental and motor performance. "Happiness is not only essential to the life of the child," she stated, "but it improves his intelligence. Here in his own little world the backward child is given the opportunity of bringing out the best that is in him. . . . This makes the work in the special school interesting and enjoyable."[18] As an example, Kordsiemon offered the following:

> A little quivering girl came up to me one morning and said, "I can't write this morning; the letters won't go right, and I don't believe I want to read either."
> I said, "Would you like to take this reed basket and go out in the yard and work awhile sitting on the bench under a tree?" She took the reed (this was work she liked to do) and sat out of doors until all the wrinkles were smoothed out and the trouble blown away. After a time she came back and was able to "make the letters go right."[19]

Not all reports on special class environments expressed such optimism. V.V. Anderson, a doctor who worked for the National Committee for Mental Hygiene, surveyed dozens of special classes across the country and concluded that "school authorities all too frequently see in the special class only a chance to segregate a greater or lesser number of the children . . . to remove from the wheels of the educational machine a certain amount of grit that disturbs the smoothness of its running gear." He argued that "too often it was obvious that there was little or no purpose in view in the training given. Weeks and months of a defective child's time might be taken up on the making of a basket or the weaving of a rug, or in doing many things that would never lead to self-support." He said such activities kept children and teachers busy but demonstrated "very little thought and attention" to their ultimate usefulness.[20]

Such anecdotes and critiques reinforced widespread concern in the early twentieth century about mental disability as an inherited, fixed trait deserving of contempt. Special classes for mentally "defective" children generated significant suspicion from much of the public and great skepticism from school leaders. These classes also symbolized the uncertainty and often desperate hopes of families and neighborhoods. Yet many of the earliest special class teachers such as Elizabeth Daniels and Harriet Lyman in Boston and Elizabeth Farrell in New York wrote powerfully and positively about their experiences with students. Teachers and students alike faced great challenges and frustrations yet apparently experienced a wonderful joy and sense of accomplishment at their achievements in their generally smaller, more individualized classrooms.

Regardless of their reputation—and it was certainly a complicated one—special classes proved to be of such value that all over the country they quickly

expanded. Created and sustained by interwoven drives for social control, operational efficiency, and individualized pedagogy, the special class remained
the primary instructional setting for children with mental disability until the
1980s. Teachers, parents, administrators, and students thus forged the notion
of a truly *special* education for children with disabilities. In decisive and fundamental ways, the particular abilities and/or perspectives of mentally disabled
children separated this branch of public education from traditional school operations. The special class, along with other specialized instructional settings,
constituted the basis for the growing mini-empire of public special education
for children with disabilities in the United States.

PROFESSIONAL DEVELOPMENT FOR SPECIAL EDUCATORS

The expanded programs in special education meant that more and more
teachers were becoming "special educators." Who were these teachers? By
the 1920s, across the country they numbered in the thousands. Discussions about what kind of teacher—and person—could best oversee a special class dominated much of the conversation about such classes. In his
classic 1924 text on special education, J. E. Wallace Wallin suggested the
following qualities as necessary and appropriate: "buoyancy, optimism, and
sympathy . . . humanity, patience, cheerfulness . . . constitutionally euphoric
and patient. . . . The special-class teacher must be able to meet defeat and disappointment with a smile. . . . She must be able to get joy and inspiration from
small accomplishments and promises of success."[21] Such idealistic assertions
abounded in the special class literature on teaching in the special classes, as did
direct advice on appropriate classroom conduct. E. R. Johnstone, for example,
cautioned:

> The teacher of defectives must use few and simple words so that
> she may be understood and when she gets an unexpected answer
> she should investigate to see if she herself is not to blame. She must
> define things in terms which are familiar to her children. She must
> have a voice that is pleasing to the ear. She must never scold. She
> must have a great heart full of sympathy.[22]

Ada Fitts, the Director of Special Classes in Boston during the early 1920s,
echoed comments similar to those of Wallin and Johnstone, adding that "a
sense of humor will help out in many a situation." *The Boston Way* summarized

such ideals best by saying that "the supreme need of one who would teach or train a little child is the power to put oneself in his place" and meet the child wherever he or she needed to be met.[23]

Educators who conducted training programs for special class teachers spoke of the seriousness and importance of the work. School systems from Boston to Los Angeles offered professional development lectures and workshops for special class teachers. Teacher training schools as well as many of the institutions for the mentally disabled offered longer programs leading to special class certification. James Riggs, principal of the State Normal and Training School in Oswego, New York, explained that his institution's year-long course, which admitted only licensed teachers, would "prepare teachers who are able to organize classes of children, plan their work, train their teachers, and then supervise a series of such classes."[24] In addition to psychology and methods classes, this course of study included a "study of society" class that placed special class work in a broader social context. By 1920, similar courses, both for licensed and preservice teachers, were commonplace. Another teacher support initiative used nationwide prepared "visiting teachers" to provide special support and guidance to teachers in delivering special class instruction. The "visiting teacher" was in fact a special education consultant or specialist whose skills included those of "the combined social worker and artistic teacher." She would work with the permanent teacher on a temporary basis, collaborating with the teacher, the child, and the child's family to enhance instructional opportunities.[25] Such rigorous, specialized preparation and support led to a distinct camaraderie and fellowship among special class teachers. As in Boston, some formed "clubs." Elsewhere, special staff within school districts engaged in constant cooperative curriculum planning.[26]

Special class teachers needed positive reinforcement because the status of the classes and their teachers within large school systems was uncertain at best. The teachers' specialized training certainly testified to the difficulty of their work. Even so, that difficulty—along with the low status of the children and their existence on the margins of public education—made the special class undesirable or unworthy in the eyes of many. Parents of the children themselves often shared such attitudes. Some parents refused to allow their child's placement into a special class. Boston school superintendent Edwin Seaver reported in 1903: "there is need of some care and delicacy in dealing with parents of these unfortunate children." The problem persisted in Boston for decades.[27] The Ottumwa, Iowa, school superintendent noted that "sensitive parents" initially resisted placement of their child in the "dummy room" and that parents "whose mental condition is more like that of their children" resisted permitting special class enrollment. Anna Kordsiemon, the special class supervisor from Quincy, Illinois, observed that "in the important task of overcoming the objection of parents to the special class much depends upon the tact and personality of the person with whom the parent has the interview." Most officials involved with special classes asserted confidently that if parents had a proper understanding of the classes' value and if the "child is happy and is able to display some accomplishments and some successes, however small they may be, the parents are satisfied." Home visits by teachers and constant communication between parents and teachers also eased parental anxiety about the special class setting.[28]

As special education grew in size and its curriculum became more sophisticated, the professional training and development of special education teachers relied more extensively on formal teacher education programs. Teacher training institutions focused primarily on training teachers for the special classes for the mentally disabled; other teachers received training in the institutions for the deaf and for the blind. By the 1930s, however, different approaches had developed, including specialized training by individual school districts and special clinics and workshops held at universities or residential institutions.

The professional journals that constantly addressed topics in the teaching of special education proved especially important in efforts to advance special education. Articles advising on best practices, teaching strategies, processes of identification, and working with parents and other social service agencies appeared in both the general education periodicals such as *Educational Review*, *Peabody Journal of Education*, and *Journal of Education* as well as in newly established specialized journals, most notably the *Journal of Exceptional Children*. Such articles typically came from college professors, school administrators, directors of special education programs, and certainly teachers in the field. For example, journals published articles on methods to diagnose and address reading difficulties; on strategies to work more effectively with "maladjusted" children, deaf–blind children, and "delicate" children; and on the nature of special education teaching or approaches to navigating the increasingly complex world of special education within larger school systems. The increased attention to these issues not only confirmed the rising importance of special education within public schooling but also encouraged greater camaraderie, support, and collaboration among those who self-identified as special educators.[29]

OTHER SPECIALIZED PUBLIC SCHOOL SETTINGS:
CLASSES FOR "DELINQUENTS"

Between 1900 and 1920 in the United States, the number as well as the diversity of special education settings in public school systems increased significantly. More children entered public schools in specialized, segregated settings, partly because of compulsory education laws but also due to more sophisticated and precise methodologies for the identification and treatment of specific disabilities. Educators created specialized classes for truant or "delinquent" pupils, students who were partially deaf or blind, children with speech impairments, and students with chronic illnesses or other physical disabilities.

The presence of students who behave "inappropriately" in class, or who don't bother to show up at all, has attracted the attention of teachers and school administrators for as long as there have been schools. The notion that such misbehavior could be a function of disability, however, is a relatively recent idea, and one still not fully accepted by many. Perhaps more than any other disabling condition, "emotional disturbance" or "behavioral disorder" generates a great deal of consternation and skepticism on the part of those who struggle to identify and adapt to it.

The history of how schools have defined and addressed behavioral disorders reflects their complicated and subjective nature. Boston opened its intermediate schools in 1838 as a means of isolating the immigrant "ruffians" and "street urchins" who, presumably, required the benefits of public education but posed a danger to younger, native children. Cleveland, New York, and Indianapolis first used ungraded classes to target students considered "incorrigible" because of truancy or misbehavior in class. The students' academic performance was a secondary issue. Boston established a Parental School in 1895, four years before it opened its first special class. The school was designed to provide strict oversight and socialization for "miscreant" public school students who previously had been sent to a juvenile prison on an island in Boston Harbor. In all these urban special schools, officials identified potential students largely on the basis of their law-breaking or disruptive behavior.[30] For example, Olive Jones of Public School 120 in New York City, a building dedicated to teaching "juvenile delinquents," identified four "distinct types of boy who find their way in to Public School 120 because the patience of teachers or parents or both has been exhausted." These included "the merely naughty boy," the "temperamentally difficult boy," "the boy with the criminal tendency," and "the truant, of the 'wanderlust' tendency." The conflation of "incorrigibility" with other disabling conditions—cognitive as well as physical—and the recognition of the effects of broader social and environmental conditions on behavior and social pathology muddied the waters even more. The construct of "defective delinquent" emerged early in the twentieth century as a way of capturing this complexity.[31]

Not surprisingly, settings for such children therefore varied widely. School districts, often working with municipal or state governments, organized separate classes, separate day schools, residential schools, and structured after-school programs in order to confine "incorrigible" children and impose some direction on them. After its opening in 1895 the Boston Parental School struggled with its programs, purpose, and identity. The city then experimented with a small number of "disciplinary day classes," which lasted only a few years. By 1915 Boston had settled on a Disciplinary Day School that met state guidelines but also provided the structured, segregated program that city leaders and local educators demanded.[32] New York and Virginia established residential institutions for "defective delinquents," separated from public schools yet focused on the education and resocialization of children labeled as "dangerous," "obstreperous," "vicious," or "ungovernable."[33]

As with special classes for the mentally retarded, most educators argued for a particular kind of teacher in these settings. "It is of primary importance," wrote J. E. W. Wallin, "that these classes be placed in charge of teachers, preferably men for boys, who, besides having all the [standard] qualifications . . . should possess wholesome, robust personalities, and a spirit of unaffected camaraderie which will enable them to win the pupils and become virtally [sic] interested in their welfare. . . . The teaching job is not merely that of providing a literary and industrial arts program . . . but of developing ideals, lofty ambitions, and a proper morale." Along with academic and vocational training many of these settings emphasized organized sports as well as work that would generate income for the school.[34]

Eventually the nonresidential disciplinary class or day school emerged as the common model for public school systems. Most were segregated by sex. Children in these settings, unlike those in residential institutions, had relatively little involvement with crime but still exhibited truant, aggressive, disobedient, or other negative behaviors in the regular school setting. The classes in such specialized settings emphasized traditional academic grade work combined with extensive vocational or industrial training and organized activities designed to teach teamwork and self-discipline. Unfortunately, the few records we have of daily life in such settings comes not from students but from teachers, supervising administrators, or other persons with a vested interest in making the schools look good. The few criticisms of such public school settings mentioned overcrowded conditions and inconsistent results as few children assigned to these settings ever returned to the regular grades.[35]

Even so, a persistent tone of hope and optimism entered into the public discourse regarding "incorrigible" and delinquent children. Advocates for such students called for a combination of medical, educational, judicial, and familial interventions to address what was a complex problem. Franklin Hoyt, Chief Justice of the Children's Court in New York City, cited his court's efforts to tend to thousands of children every year. Courts in Chicago and Denver were similarly busy. "Of course these children are not all delinquent," Hoyt wrote. "About one-half are neglected and are brought before the court because their parents have sinned, either actively or passively, and because they have been denied their inherent right to a normal and decent home." Hoyt used a Biblical passage to describe the Court's work: "I delivered the poor that cried, and the fatherless, and him that had none to help him—The cause which I knew not, I search out."[36] Edgar Shimer, a district superintendent of schools in New York, argued that any child could be reached. "The very substance of the things hoped for by us, in this forward movement to reclaim lost souls, lies in our unwavering faith that such reclamation is possible and that we can help to make it actual . . . as exprest [sic] by Ralph Waldo Emerson, 'In the muck and scum of things, there is something always sings.'" Shimer paid respects to those "numerous principals and teachers, whose passion for perfection prompts them unerringly toward the reconstruction and salvation of the imperfect." Such a romantic view of child reform could survive and operate beside a school system's effort to keep "vicious" children away from the regular classrooms because both the romantic and the realist felt segregating "delinquent children" was valuable and necessary.[37]

OTHER SETTINGS: DAY SCHOOLS AND CLASSES FOR THE DEAF AND BLIND

The strong presence and reputation of residential institutions for the deaf and the blind throughout the United States by no means prevented public school systems from educating children with hearing and/or vision impairments. Following the establishment of the Boston Day School for Deaf Mutes within the Boston public school system in 1869, urban school districts across the country began to offer individual classes and day school programs for children who were partially or totally deaf. Most such schools used the oralist approach and included classes in lipreading. Pennsylvania opened a day school in Erie in 1874 and the state of Wisconsin had a system of such schools by the 1880s. For children who were partially blind, public school classes (typically known as "sight-saving" classes or classes for the "semi-blind") and day schools for the blind followed soon after. Chicago started a class for totally blind children in 1900; Boston and Cleveland initiated the first sight-saving classes in 1913. Educators found day classes an economical way to provide a state-supported education for deaf and blind children who couldn't gain admittance to overcrowded institutions.[38] Public school settings were also less isolating. Historian of the deaf Harry Best noted that "with the deaf child attendance at the day school does not make him a stranger in his own home . . . while there is kept alive on all sides a feeling of family responsibility . . . [and] is more acceptable to the child's parents."[39]

The nonresidential classes for children with hearing impairments in public schools gained widespread popularity as successful models of the oralist approach to deaf education. Boston's day school, renamed the Horace Mann School for the Deaf in 1877, achieved a national and international reputation for excellence in deaf education. It constantly hosted visitors, observers, and others interested in the work. The school's curriculum reflected a belief that deaf students needed a balanced education, one that embodied both standard academic course work and extensive manual and vocational training that could lead to useful employment. The highlight of education at Horace Mann was Visible Speech, a method of study for deaf students devised by Alexander Graham Bell's father and widely and fervently promoted by the son. The method involved the use of lipreading for communication and aimed to prepare deaf students for more effective integration into the mainstream of society.

Although the Horace Mann School segregated its students in a building separate from other public schools in the city, school officials supported the integration of deaf persons in society. This integration was the central feature of the oralist approach and one that challenged the more traditional view of the sanctity and viability of an independent deaf culture and community. In terms of curriculum and mission, day schools around the country looked up to the Horace Mann School as the embodiment of the integrationist ideal for deaf persons. By the early 1900s, more than a hundred cities and more than twenty states had day school services for deaf students. Still, traditional supporters of sign language and the manualist perspective roundly criticized such settings, as did others who urged combining the two methods.[40]

The segregated nature of their daily school life constituted a central feature of the lives of children within day schools and classes for the deaf. The highly specialized nature of their curriculum with regard to texts and methodology, and the unique training and skills of their teachers, set such schools apart from standard public school classrooms. Separate classrooms, and often (as in the case of the Horace Mann School) separate buildings, permitted few opportunities for children with hearing impairments to interact with their hearing peers. The only times deaf and hearing students commonly interacted was in advanced industrial or vocational training in school workshops where deaf students could rely on lipreading skills to communicate sufficiently.[41]

Interestingly, lipreading classes for partially deaf students represent one of the earliest examples of the "resource room" or "pull-out" instruction still common today. Most children in the day schools had hearing deficiencies that prevented even minimal involvement in regular classroom work. Lipreading classes in some school districts took place several times a week to train children in this skill so that they could remain in the regular classroom most of the week. Educators argued that segregation for specialized lipreading (or "speech reading") programs was fundamental to the successful education of the child with hearing impairments. Imogen Palen, a teacher of a public school lipreading class, painted a vivid and sad picture of the struggles of partially deaf children in the regular classroom. Poor hearing could lead to poor academic performance, and Palen argued that typically the child "is blamed for dullness and inattention. After a time he accepts as true these statements of his superiors that he is stupid and careless and he ceases to try for success." She asserted that consistent attendance for a few hours a week in a segregated lipreading program would allow the child to succeed in the regular classroom. With such special instruction, his "ambition is revived and he usually shows improvement in class standing from the first of the work."[42]

Public school programs for children with vision impairments primarily served children who had at least some vision. Totally blind students usually attended residential institutions for their formal education. Public schools employed two models: the day schools and the "sight-saving" classes. Day schools, which were much fewer in number, served primarily children without any sight who lived within the school district. The sight-saving classes targeted children who had some vision. In fact, the foremost purpose of these classes was to "save" whatever residual vision the child had. In many school districts there may have been some overlap or even a merger of the day school and sight-saving concepts.[43]

As in the segregated settings for deaf children, teachers of classes for students with vision impairments followed the regular school curriculum as much as possible. Of course they used appropriate technological and environmental adjustments. In the day schools, raised print (either New York point or Braille) for textbooks constituted the fundamental adaptation. Specially trained teachers in these schools also incorporated into the curriculum physical fitness, manual training, and music. Many day schools also made special arrangements to help transport the students from home to school and back. Although day schools cost much less to operate than residential institutions and allowed children to remain with their families, critics worried the schools offered fewer specialized opportunities and resources than did institutions for the blind. Moreover, blind students were an awkward presence in an almost exclusively seeing public school environment. Residential facilities probably provided their students more help and support.[44]

Nonetheless, sight-saving classes proved very popular and enjoyed widespread support among school personnel and also reform groups interested in the prevention of blindness. Gordon Berry of the National Committee for the Prevention of Blindness hailed sight-saving classes as a necessary component of public schools that ensured improved overall health and academic performance for blind students across the country. Berry also called for thorough medical inspection of all students. This practice became commonplace by the 1920s and included attention to students with potential vision problems. He advised teachers to be on the lookout for possible vision defects: "for instance, scowling, squinting, headaches, reading matter held at an improper distance from the eye, inflammation, pus formation, inability to see the blackboard clearly . . . cross-eye, weariness after study, bloodshot eyes, or crusty lids."[45]

Once identified, students placed in sight-saving classes benefited from specially trained teachers, many of whom had been educated at residential institutions. The standard curriculum as well as physical exercise, music, and manual training aimed to preserve and strengthen any vision a student might have. Sensory-motor work, including painting and drawing, basket weaving, and piano tuning, held special importance for younger children. Typically sight-saving classes provided a radically altered classroom environment designed to place as little stress as possible on their students' remaining eyesight. There were special lights, soft or muted color schemes, large-print books, magnifying glasses, dictaphones, and seats and desks that adjusted to a child's optimal positioning. Teachers relied heavily on oral instruction. Such classes typically remained small to meet the varying needs of each child. In 1913, Superintendent Franklin Dyer of the Boston public schools commented that "every case is different.... The school attempts to train each child according to its [*sic*] defect."[46]

Sight-saving classes for blind children had both supporters and detractors. One argument in favor of day schools was that thanks to the blind children's presence in the regular public school system "the public in general becomes better acquainted with their possibilities [including their academic talents] and with their limitations."[47] Conversely, Franklin Dyer lamented the isolation of Boston's one (at that time) sight-saving class, and another Boston administrator argued that "when [the vision impaired student] mingles with other children and he recites in their class rooms such nicknames as 'blinky' and 'blindy' disappear."[48] As a result, many school districts across the country experimented with careful articulation of sight-saving classes with regular classes and combined instruction as much as possible. Ultimately, educators hoped that sight-saving classes and potential interaction with sighted children would help a vision-impaired student "free [himself] from mannerisms, a feeling of dependence, morbid consciousness of his handicap, and the abnormal craving for compassion."[49]

SPECIALIZED SETTINGS: SPEECH IMPROVEMENT

Another cluster of disabilities that proved especially problematic in a formal school setting were speech disorders. By the early 1900s, there existed a better medical understanding of the origins and treatment of speech difficulties. Stuttering or "stammering" was the most prevalent of these disabling conditions; others included lisping, mutism, aphonia, "undeveloped" speech, "backwardness in all oral work," "baby talk," and "nasality." Teachers worried about affected students' social and academic problems. A student's inability to speak clearly and confidently could negatively affect performance in regular classrooms that still required considerable amounts of recitation. It could also lead to cruel mimicry by her peers and affect her mental state as well as her social skills. Interestingly, speech disorders unexpectedly affected large numbers of students: the Detroit public schools expressed surprise at the number of students who were "discovered" to have defective speech, and by 1925 speech improvement classes had become the single largest program of special education in terms of enrollment in the Boston public schools.[50]

Typical programs for speech improvement took the form of "pull-out" sessions, where a student would leave his classroom for a few hours a week to obtain speech therapy and training. In Chicago, such training consisted of various exercises related to "breathing . . . relaxation . . . rhythm, and . . . the development of self-confidence." This approach included five minutes of "silent deep breathing, in varying positions, and three or four minutes for silent relaxation, to gain poise."[51] Similar work occurred in Detroit and Boston, where children also learned the mechanics or "geography" of the speech organs.[52] Everywhere teachers coached youngsters in the discrete pronunciation of consonants and other problematic sounds and utilized "psychological" measures to ease tension and self-consciousness on the speaker's part and "eliminate fear and the fear of talking." For most children involved in speech improvement, the majority of their school time was spent in regular classrooms, practicing the techniques and skills learned in the "pull-out" sessions. Regular classroom teachers also provided at least some training in phonetics and in the process of speech formation.[53]

It is important to note that concerns about speech "defects" were not limited to the physiological. In an article entitled "The Need of Speech Work in the High Schools," Alma M. Bullowa of Hunter College in New York City focused on the issue of "standards." Bullowa lamented that there were "so many places—little Italy, little Russia, little Ireland, little Poland—that there is no standard of correctly spoken English. . . . It is the most difficult thing in the world for an educated adult to keep his standard—to maintain a purity of language against the corruptions of the majority in the streets. Eternal vigilance is the price of pure English!" She insisted that "there are a hundred ways of demonstrating that the voice or speech which is undesirable is habitual, but not natural, that it is no more natural than any pathological condition for the cure or correction of which the medical man is consulted." Bullowa also claimed that stuttering and stammering in fact arose from "the lack of standard" in proper English pronunciation. Wallin's survey of the St. Louis schools convinced him that "about three percent" of children in the schools there had speech defects, not including "a considerable number of cases of foreign accent, patois, or brogue." Indeed, cultural definitions of "proper" and "defective" speech were difficult for many to separate from physiological or psychological origins: "slovenliness or negligent speech" was considered every bit as "defective" as stuttering or lisping in Boston as elsewhere, as

Bullowa's strident condemnation of foreign-accented English makes perfectly clear.[54]

SPECIALIZED SETTINGS: CHRONICALLY ILL AND "CRIPPLED" CHILDREN

By the early 1900s, increasingly disability became defined as a medical problem. This change is readily apparent if we examine programs created by most public school systems during the period for children with chronic illnesses (especially tuberculosis). Educators grew increasingly aware of the presence of children in schools whose medical condition seemingly affected their academic performance and the health of other children. Public schools moved decisively to establish settings to isolate the ill and segregate the "helpless cripple." These included "open-air" or "fresh air" classes for tubercular children, special schools for children with orthopedic and other physical disabilities, and home instruction for children whose condition prevented school attendance.

The open-air or fresh-air classes arose from concerns about the presence of children in public schools whose health condition seemed dangerous to others. Usually these youngsters had communicable diseases such as tuberculosis; then-current medical practice advocated exposing tubercular children to as much fresh, cool air as possible to help improve functioning of the lungs. Once again Boston was at the forefront of special education development. The city established its first open-air class in 1908. Other cities, including Chicago, Detroit, New York, and Cleveland soon followed suit. These cities and others typically organized several such classes. In most open-air classes, students studied the standard school curriculum but at a slower pace to allow more opportunities for the afflicted children to rest and engage in stamina-building pursuits. Rooms were kept as cool as possible, and windows remained open in even the coldest weather. When necessary, students received blankets. Open-air classrooms also contained cots where children could rest as needed, and the boys and girls received constant medical monitoring. By the late 1920s most of these classes had been discontinued as air-filtering systems in schools improved and the threat of tuberculosis subsided. Moreover, many school districts offered similar, specifically tailored classes and classrooms for children with heart conditions, and Boston was one of several school systems to extend instruction to students confined for long periods of time to hospitals.[55]

During the early twentieth century, public schools began to pay much closer attention to children with physical abnormalities or disabilities. Educators labeled them "crippled" children. Compulsory education brought more of these children to the attention of the schools. These were children who previously may have been sequestered or confined by their families or admitted to a residential institution. Crippled children attracted a great deal of attention and pity. "Helpless" was a common descriptor for their assumed condition. Accordingly, public school facilities and programs for such children grew at a remarkable rate.

Even though educators recognized that crippled students could perform up to academic standards most of the time, they nonetheless championed construction of separate facilities. While acknowledging that a crippled child "learns as easily and oftentimes faster than the normal child," one author explained that because the child is "unable to go to school by himself, and he will not get there unless he is carried . . . our large cities are now furnishing special schools or classes for crippled children." By the early 1920s, Chicago had four such schools and Detroit had thirteen classes in its Leland School, which was "housed in an admirable building, specially constructed and equipped for crippled children." At the same time, Cleveland had six classes for such students and encouraged their transfer to regular classroom settings whenever possible. Nevertheless the city constructed a separate school for crippled children in the early 1920s.[56]

The educational experience for children in these settings was distinctive in many ways. To begin with, children received special transportation services to and from school, usually in "motor buses," police cars, or other officially labeled vehicles. Once at the school, boys and girls studied the standard public school curriculum, but they also received specific medical and physiological therapy for their particular conditions. Children who were physically disabled due to accidents, rickets, complications at birth, or infantile paralysis might receive wheelchairs, crutches, or braces. Furthermore, "in these schools the children are always under medical supervision. They have special desks that are fitted to them, and there are special ways of teaching them to walk. There is massage and passive exercise to bring back the use of paralyzed limbs." The Spalding School in Chicago offered "corrective gymnastics, physical rehabilitation, and vocational training . . . in cooking, sewing, printing, typewriting, cobbling, weaving (14 looms), sheet metal and woodwork. The children [also] complete the elementary course." An observer commented that the school "was planned and built exclusively for crippled children. The rooms are large, well-lighted and splendidly equipped." The Chicago schools superintendent, Peter Mortenson, proudly stated that "to open the way to happiness; to build up faith and confidence; to inspire courage and self-respect—this is the work of the schools for the handicapped."[57]

Such segregated facilities did not suit everyone. Some families found that their children simply could not cope with the physical challenges of traveling to and from school, so several school districts offered home instruction. For example Chelsea, Massachusetts, provided home instruction for a fourteen-year-old boy with a debilitating hunched back; another boy who had "weakness in his legs" since infancy; a seventh-grader with a severe case of rheumatic fever; and a nine-year-old boy whose "violent convulsions affected both his mind and body, making his case a most difficult one." Some educators also doubted the need for separate school settings for crippled children. James A. Treavor, a teacher at Grover Cleveland Junior High School in Boston, argued that "very little will be gained by isolating crippled children in a separate school unit." Another author maintained that medical "miracles" could correct all but the most serious of physical disabilities. "A crippled school for crippled children is a horrible proposition," he wrote. "Nothing is quite as vicious in the treatment of crippled children as to have them feel that they cannot associate with physical and mental normal children." Even so, supporters of such schools could see no wrong in them. "What a gratifying sight it is," extolled a New York City school administrator, "to observe boys and girls, sadly handicapped at first, gain in physical and intellectual strength so as to be happy, industrious, and self-supporting, taking their place completely with all useful citizens and bread winners!"[58]

SPECIAL EDUCATION IN THE 1930S: STRUGGLING, YET TAKING HOLD

The first three decades of the twentieth century thus witnessed remarkable structural and curricular changes in terms of public education in the United States. The impact of Progressivism was especially strong on schools, reflecting their beliefs regarding efficiency in operation, objectivist as well as scientific approaches to educational research, and more practical and child-centered approaches to classroom instruction. The "business" of public schooling emphasized effective administration, a thoughtfully organized instructional ladder leading from first through twelfth grades, specialized instruction for particular groups of students, and effective academic and vocational preparation for all students once they had graduated. During the 1920s, across the nation educators introduced middle schools in an attempt to better help students cope with the transition from elementary to high school. The Cardinal Principles of Secondary Education, issued in 1918 by the Commission on the Reorganization of Secondary Education of the National Education Association, called for a much different high school curriculum than the classical one defended by the Committee of Ten on Secondary Studies, also of the NEA, report issued a generation earlier in 1893. Instead of universal, strictly academic instruction, the Cardinal Principles encouraged a highly differentiated secondary school curriculum designed to meet the practical and vocational challenges of the modern twentieth century. This curriculum featured separate curricular tracks for students depending on their anticipated post–high school plans, an emphasis on the development of good citizenship, and preparation for a useful role in society.[59]

Progressivism in education and a stronger emphasis on school involvement in vocational preparation contributed strongly to the directions special education began to take in the 1930s. The Great Depression of the 1930s certainly strapped the resources of school districts tremendously. Special education programs suffered from inadequate resources as well as low status and morale. The gap between special education and regular education widened. Schools struggled to accommodate the rapidly increasing number of students deemed eligible for special education. Students nationwide were staying in school longer and attending high school, and students with disabilities were no exception. The opportunity to stay occupied in a secure and controlled environment appealed to all students, including those with disabilities, given the difficulty in finding paid employment. School districts thus attended to special education in the practical and vocational arena, with some engaging in high-profile construction projects to demonstrate their commitment to practical preparation for all students in the struggling economy. Many states supplemented district resources with financial aid to support special education. The result was a slowed and damaged but still significant commitment to special education programs throughout the decade.[60]

After its 1930 meeting the White House Conference committee on the handicapped had emphasized the importance and value of what it termed "vocational adjustment" for students with disabilities, including the introduction of sheltered workshops, prevocational training, and specific job training as a key aspect of what the committee referred to as "social adjustment." The committee noted such trends occurring already in urban areas while lamenting their absence "almost entirely" in rural districts. "Special education is a school administrative device by means of which children who deviate from the normal . . . can be given the kind of training they require under more favorable conditions," wrote the committee. "Gradually . . . other features, making for a complete program of vocational preparation and employment of the handi-capped are being added to the curricula." Virtually all these changes took place among older disabled children who, it was believed, could not benefit from academic work but could from industrial or vocational training.[61]

The development of special education during the 1930s, however, involved much more than mere vocational training. Indeed, city school districts across the country engaged in a great deal of mutual and self-praise regarding new developments in curricular, instructional, and socialization practices for pub-lic school children with disabilities. As special education teachers gained more experience with their students and continued developing their unique identity as special educators, they continued the process begun decades earlier of de-veloping more varied or ambitious structures for and approaches to their work. Their reports often offered detailed glimpses of life inside special education classrooms in the public schools.

One common way to spread word of practices and accomplishments in spe-cial education was for a member of a city school district's special education department to publish in a professional journal a description of special educa-tion in their particular city and school system. These reports emanated from the largest cities such as Chicago, Cleveland, Detroit, and Los Angeles as well as from medium-sized districts such as Sheboygan, Wisconsin; Des Moines, Iowa; and Paterson, New Jersey. They provided a means to share best practices and draw national attention to local success stories.

These descriptions varied somewhat in their approaches. For example, Philadelphia and Sheboygan, Wisconsin, focused on their new state-of-the-art buildings and programs for children with physical disabilities. The 1930s was a busy time for constructing such facilities; other cities, including Cleveland and Indianapolis, constructed new schools specifically geared toward "crippled" children. The Philadelphia facility, known as the Orthopedic School, boasted not only classrooms and industrial arts shops but also "inner courts" for play-ground facilities and indoor gardens. The school also housed a gymnasium, a swimming pool, separate dining and assembly rooms, and an auditorium, all designed to accommodate children using wheelchairs, crutches, braces, and other equipment that would impair their mobility in a regular school building. Sheboygan's description of its School for the Physically Handicapped focused more on how pleasing life was for the students and how much they were actually capable of doing. "Unfortunate—yes, but fortunate, too, in the happy hours which come to them in the classroom where their infirmities are largely forgotten," stated the preface to the article by Olga Zufelt. Zufelt described a bright, cheerful, lively environment where children sang, played games, acted in plays, took field trips outside the school to parks, city offices, and even a miniature golf course. Children were "also trained in the social graces" and received visits from a wide range of civic groups. "Every child in school is happy to be there," she claimed. "It is a place where parents want their children to be because of its particular advantages. They realize that they are fortunate to have compatible surroundings, where intelligence, understanding, and science minister to their every need."[62]

Some cities ventured to tell a larger story of the entire special education system supported by their public schools. Descriptive articles from Los Angeles, Detroit, Milwaukee, and Chicago reveal that each city had its special education programs structured in a similar fashion, with separate classes or facilities for children with mental retardation, speech impairments, chronic illness or "anemia," vision and hearing impairments, "maladjustments," and cardiac conditions. Each provided statistics on the number of classes and enrollment. Each noted the value of small class sizes, well-trained teachers, and segregated facilities. A report on Cleveland's Thomas A. Edison School "for Problem Boys" also tried to be reassuring (perhaps suspiciously so) regarding the comportment at the school: "An atmosphere of orderly co-operation and good nature is apparent throughout the building. There is little disturbance in the classrooms. Boys and teachers are on friendly terms and get on without friction. Discipline problems are rare." While positive in tone and rich in detail about facilities, processes of identification, and elements of the curriculum, many of these program descriptions lacked any specific descriptions of life inside these isolated settings.[63]

Other cities, however, offered descriptions not only of the program particulars but also of much of the atmosphere and characteristics of the settings themselves. A report out of Paterson, New Jersey emphasized the value that special education in public schools brought to the quality of life for its students over that provided by residential institutions. There, classes for a wide range of categories of "unfortunates" were all held in School No. 2, to which "anyone interested is always a welcome visitor." Although acknowledging that "the asylum has its advantages," Frank Rich, the principal of the school, noted the institutions' "serious disadvantages [which] have always interfered with the general education of defectives." Foremost was the absence of a natural and authentic home and family life: "It isn't simply the anguish that comes from separating child from parent. . . . A better psychology helps us to understand more clearly just why it is so bad to take a child out of a fair to good home . . . and why so many institution children are never quite normal, often rather queer." Rich went on to state that living at home provided children with a stronger emotional and intellectual life and that a public school education can offer a more personalized education. "Nothing can ever take the place of the good, old-fashioned home, with a devoted, painstaking mother, a jovial, strong-minded father, and the good-natured sacrifice and rivalry of brothers and sisters. . . . Fortunately our school system makes that possible even with pupils seriously handicapped."[64]

Rich's article contained some vivid accounts of the difficulties of teaching children with special needs. "Can you imagine learning to make a perfect imitation of the cry of some strange animal you have never heard, with your own ears stopped so that you cannot hear the voice of the one who is instructing you nor the sounds you make yourself," he asked in discussing deaf children. "Then there is the problem of using verbs in various modes and tenses, and modifiers and connectives in a world that consists wholly of nouns and pronouns. It is difficult, but not impossible . . . we shall be glad to show you the work in operation." He also told of "a boy paralyzed on one side, blind, and seriously retarded mentally, whom we have trained to service candy vending machines on several corners. . . . His success for the future is assured. If we can do this much for him, we ought to be able to do a great deal more for others."[65]

With the growth of special education, teachers and curriculum developers took note of innovative ideas regarding the education of children with disabilities. Some of these ideas focused on a specific category of disability. Others cut across such categories, advocating the use of subjects such as art, poetry, drama, music, and special projects for children with any kind of disability. Drawing on progressive education ideas in hands-on education and project-based learning, these novel approaches took advantage of the assumed benefits of affective and psychomotor instruction for disabled children, especially those with mental retardation. The belief that activities that engaged children, that integrated different subjects, and that could lead to some practical benefit were of significant value to children with disabilities gained wide acceptance among many practitioners.

One popular approach was to engage students with mild to moderate mental retardation in re-creating everyday businesses and offices in their classroom as an ongoing project. In Mabel Davison's classroom in Washington, DC, students became interested in building a post office after discussing the importance of mail at Christmas and on Valentine's Day. "There was a babble of voices—and enthusiasm for the undertaking ran high," Davison reported. A field trip to the post office led to a highly detailed project that required listing necessary materials, planning and constructing a "building" in the classroom, and identifying personal qualifications of the class postmaster. The project involved a series of lessons and activities that incorporated reading, writing, speech, math, manual and fine arts, social studies, and character training.[66] Katherine Lynch's class in New York City underwent a similar process when constructing a grocery store in the classroom. Ms. Lynch identified positive outcomes similar to those named by Ms. Davison: they "live through an experience that would develop them mentally, physically, socially, and emotionally. They learn to adjust to classmates, strange but official adults, new situations. . . . They learn to meet defeat and success. . . . *In fact they learn how to get along with forces, materials, machines, and people*" (italics in the original).[67] Another school, this one in Detroit, organized several classes and teachers in a buildingwide project on transportation. The activities featured field trips, research, a variety of integrated content-related activities, and the transformation of parts of classrooms into "real-word" facilities. A special capstone component of the Detroit project was a mock radio broadcast describing various transportation experiences.[68]

Engaging students in poetry, drama, and accessible literature constituted another favored approach, especially in efforts to develop affective and imaginative aspects of the child. Augusta Feiner, another Detroit special class teacher, saw drama as a means to strengthen weaker aspects of the "dull child." Contending that these children tended to be shy, unimaginative, and awkward, with "slovenly diction" and poor reading skills, Feiner proclaimed that "dramatization is also worth while for the mentally retarded child for then he can play a new exciting part in life and can rise above the inadequate person he knows himself to be."[69] Vesta Thompson of Portsmouth, New Hampshire, expressed a more positive view of her students in describing her use of poetry to excite their imagination. She related how she used the poem "Hiawatha" to have her students close their eyes and see with their minds. One child, Ruth, struggled with the activity, and Thompson provided a detailed description of how she walked Ruth through the process, assisted by the other children. "'Can you see [the baby] now? Try real hard.' There was momentary silence, and then Ruth cried: 'O, yes, yes! Now I see him, I see him.' . . . Her imagination had at last been awakened, and led to the proper channel."[70] Other strategies included the practice of "supplementation," where students would become engaged in practical application of content—for example, auto mechanics to supplement science class—or in enrichment activities that extended beyond the normal curriculum and generated interest in a subject that couldn't be generated in the regular curriculum.[71]

STUDENTS WITH DISABILITIES IN THE ONE-ROOM SCHOOL

While public school systems in large cities created special classes and day schools for disabled children, the thousands of one-room schools and other small, simple educational settings had little choice but to take a different approach to the presence and demands of disabled youngsters. In such schools, smaller classes and more flexible classroom structures and practices allowed teachers and administrators to adapt more readily to work with children with special educational needs. Lack of financial and other resources significantly restricted the options of rural and small-town schools to provide special education. Such schools also had limited access to teachers trained to teach the disabled. Mechanisms for formal identification of disability often did not exist in small school districts, partly because the number of children who might potentially qualify was too low to invest the time, effort, and money in testing for disabilities. Although small districts were certainly aware of developments in special education in the larger cities of the United States, small schools had little need to develop complex special education programming. Moreover, many states explicitly required that "all deaf, dumb, blind and idiotic children coming under the provisions of the [compulsory education] law . . . be sent to the proper state schools for such children." Such policies excused rural and small-town districts from attending to students with obvious disabilities.[72]

Even so, it is possible to gain some understanding of how teachers and students experienced disability in these small school settings. In such schools, there were clearly wide differences among students. A state report issued by Indiana around 1911 noted that the course of study in fact "existed for the child. . . . The child must not be overlooked. His present knowledge, his needs, and his possibilities must all be considered. . . . It is important that the school fix the habit of doing well whatever is undertaken." The report recommended the omission of the "less important" if the full curriculum couldn't be covered. A more detailed description comes from Indiana's Decatur County, which likely captures the status and practices of rural schools throughout the nation around the turn of the century:

> Classes were not graded one, two, three, etc. at first. A pupil was in a certain reader, or to the word "unique" in the speller, or on a certain page of the arithmetic.... These rural youngsters profited by listening to the older ones recite up front on the recitation bench and seeing things on the blackboard for other classes.... Often times faster pupils helped slower ones.... On the first day of schol [sic] the teachers had the pupils to sit down, and then said, "Now we don't have any idiots or half-idiots here and WE ARE GOING TO HAVE SCHOOL." It worked and they had a good school.[73]

By the late 1930s children with identifiable disabilities in rural schools were attracting considerably more attention. "The time ... has come when the Council [for Exceptional Children] should make some definite effort towards the improvement of the education of those several millions of exceptional children who are found in smaller centers and in rural areas," stated educational psychologist Samuel Laycock in 1935. In his address to the International Council for Exceptional Children, Laycock advised the Council to appoint committees to study the "problem."[74] In fact, the issues were readily apparent. Helen Heffernan of the California State Department of Education observed: "Naturally, the rural school, where financial support is meager, where teachers are relatively less well-trained, where pupil population is scattered over large areas, and where the attitude of the public may be apathetic or indifferent, is *bringing up the rear*" (emphasis in the original) in providing special education.[75]

The widespread assumption that a significant portion of students in these schools were in fact disabled is borne out by looking at some descriptions of teachers of their classrooms. Lily Peter, a teacher and principal in a small school in Arkansas, described her work with Eleanor Lee, a "little girl about eleven years old who had infantile paralysis as a baby, and whose left arm is shriveled and the hand almost completely paralyzed as a result." Ms. Peter taught the child how to use one finger of her left hand to play simple piano pieces; Eleanor in turn taught the piece to another child.[76] Mary Bryan taught in a one-room school in Tennessee where she experienced "quite a few problems.... A backward pupil increases difficulties by requiring extra coaching."[77] She described others of all ages who were well below grade level academically. Another Tennessee teacher told of "two of my children who are not well adjusted" who "work with me on this corner seat. Here we are not close enough to the other children to disturb them in their work and yet we are not so far away as to appear a separate group."[78]

Indiana teacher Anna Draper experienced similar conditions. She provided medical attention to Harold, a first-grader "who is always sick." She had to administer medicine, "watch his diet," and try "to keep him awake long enough to teach him the things that the other children are learning." Another child "is a nervous wreck and is in no condition to learn while at school."[79] Wanda Hitch's small school in rural western Indiana had a ten-year-old third-grade girl whose "mentality is below normal, but the other children do not realize it. She has a very irritating personality . . . a 'chronic complainer.' Previous to this year no teacher has tried to help her."[80] Carmel Jett taught for seven months in a one-room school in the hills of Kentucky. On the first day of school she had fifty students, thirty seats, and students aged 5 to 16 in grades one through seven. Her student Juanita "was incorrigible to the last white hair"; Kathleen had "dreamy eyes and [a] quick, sensitive mind"; Virgil was "not an angel, but an angle." While it would be impossible to know for certain, such children might well have found themselves labeled exceptional or disabled in the more rigid and disability-sensitive world of a large public school system.[81]

Identifying children with disabilities thus assumed a primary role in bringing effective special education to rural areas. Doing so began with the teacher. "If the classroom teacher can be educated to recognize the types of cases and to know some of the specialized techniques required by the exceptional child's peculiar problem, she could give at least some of the attention needed," advised California administrator Helen Heffernan. "With all the disadvantages which the rural school may possess, perhaps it prevents one of the worst errors into which we have fallen in the treatment of our exceptional children; namely, complete segregation from the normal social group." Heffernan also recommended a corps of teachers to work statewide in identifying disabled children, special summer workshops for rural teachers, and financial as well as professional support from the state government and special supervisors in special education or health education. She also recommended using more of the "traveling clinics" that had been in existence since the early 1920s.[82]

Investigation by medical and psychological professionals complemented the efforts of teachers and state school officials. Winona, Minnesota, organized a school clinic that worked with parents, homes, and the local parent–teacher association to identify children with disabilities. On occasion they encountered resistance from parents to such a diagnosis, but most parents reportedly welcomed the work. Rural Allegheny County in Pennsylvania worked with the local Lion's Club and the county medical society to identify students with visual impairments and to supply schools with necessary materials to teach them. The collaborative and cooperative nature of the work was essential, with "educational forces, health officers, probation departments, and welfare agencies united for concerted action to prevent social and personal maladjustment" in rural regions of the United States.[83]

The limited record indicates that rural teachers and administrators accepted as natural a classroom that could range in size from a few children to dozens, from boys and girls aged 3 or 4 to young men and women having just entered adulthood. Rural educators understood that academic ability varied tremendously according to a child's natural capabilities, home life, and experience with formal or even informal schooling in general. Rural and small-town teachers certainly noted those children who were unusually capable, or who struggled academically, or who were particularly able—or unable—to tolerate the typical stultifying school day in what were all too often extremely uncomfortable conditions. Yet most accommodated and adjusted as best they could. They relied on the practices and experiences of generations before them. Even by the 1930s, most rural youngsters did not yet not encounter the specialization and segregation that was beginning to define the school experiences of literally hundreds of thousands of urban children with exceptional needs.[84]

On the eve of the Second World War, then, public schools across the country had become more deeply committed to a special education for children with disabilities. Doing so involved not only school policies and classroom practices but collaborative work with medical professionals, social service agencies, and, increasingly, with parents and families themselves. From 1940 through the 1950s, special education continued its long yet seemingly inexorable process of development and entrenchment in the public sphere, encountering heightened interest and scrutiny from a broader public. The next chapter will explore disability's growing visibility in American society and special education's consequent expansion as well as its growing need for self-promotion—and self-defense—as it became an even more significant part of the lives of disabled children.

NOTES

1. Cited in Seymour Sarason and John Doris, *Educational Handicap, Public Policy, and Social History: A Broadened Perspective on Mental Retardation* (New York, 1979), 275.

2. Joseph L. Tropea, "Bureaucratic Order and Special Children: Urban Schools, 1890s–1940s," *History of Education Quarterly* 27 (Spring 1987): 32, 36.

3. See Margret Winzer, *The History of Special Education: From Isolation to Integration* (Washington, DC, 1993), 320–22; R. C. Scheerenberger, *A History of Mental Retardation* (Baltimore, MD, 1983), 129–30; J. E. Wallace Wallin, *The Education of Handicapped Children* (Boston, MA, 1924), 37–38; Robert L. Osgood, *For "Children Who Vary from the Normal Type": Special Education in Boston 1838–1930* (Washington, DC, 2000), 75–76.

4. Cited in Osgood, *For "Children Who Vary from the Normal Type,"* 73–75.

5. Cited in Osgood, *For "Children Who Vary from the Normal Type,"* 88–89.

6. Cited in Sarason and Doris, *Educational Handicap*, 300; Tropea, "Bureaucratic Order and Special Children," 32; Osgood, *For "Children Who Vary from the Normal Type,"* 92.

7. "Defectives," *Journal of Education* 93 (February 24, 1921): 212; George Bliss, "President's Address: The Need of a Better Social Conscience," *Indiana Bulletin* 120 (March 1920): 26; James T. Byers, "Provision for the Feeble-Minded," *Proceedings and Papers of the Indiana State Teachers Association*, 64th Annual Session, 1917, 169.

8. Meta Anderson, *Education of Defectives in the Public Schools* (Yonkers-on-Hudson, NY, 1917), ix; E. R. Johnstone, "President's Address: The Functions of the Special Class," *Addresses and Proceedings of the National Education Association*, 1908, 1115–16. See also the series of articles by various Indiana school superintendents in *Indiana Bulletin* 180 (March 1930): 62–81; and Thomas D. Wood, "Discussion," *Addresses and Proceedings of the National Education Association*, 1903, 1003–4.

9. Tropea, "Bureaucratic Order and Special Children," passim; Marvin Lazerson, "The Origins of Special Education," in *Special Education Policies: Their History, Implementation, and Finance*, ed. Jay G. Chambers and William T. Hartman (Philadelphia, PA, 1983), 15–33. See also Stanley P. Davies, *Social Control of the Mentally Deficient* (New York, 1930), 293–323, and Osgood, *For "Children Who Vary from the Normal Type,"* 57–59.

10. Wallin, *Education of Handicapped Children*, 37–38; Davies, *Social Control of the Mentally Deficient*, 299–300. The terminology for classes dedicated to the education of children with mental disabilities varied widely. The early undifferentiated classes never really shared a common label; the first that "took" was Boston's "ungraded" class, designed for older immigrant children but actually serving a wide range of disabilities. Classes specifically designed for children with mental disabilities were typically called "special" classes, although "ungraded" and "opportunity" also were used.

11. Osgood, *For "Children Who Vary from the Normal Type,"* 131–33; Elizabeth Farrell, cited in Sarason and Doris, *Educational Handicap*, 297–98; Margaret Knox, "The Principal's Point of View of the Selection of Children for Special Classes," *Journal of the National Education Association* 2 (1917): 872–73. For a detailed description of the evaluation process used by Dr. Jelly, see Knox, 878–79.

12. Arthur B. Lord, "The Mentally Retarded," *Journal of Education* 107 (May 28, 1928): 635; Bertha M. Luckey, A. H. Sutherland, and Frank Cody, "The Practical Value of Psychological Tests—Do They Find the Bright and Dull Pupils?" *Journal of the National Education Association* 3 (1918): 388–94; Herman H. Young, "Experiments in Public Schools," *Indiana Bulletin* 136 (March 1924): 26; William R. Comings, "Are Mentality Tests on Right Lines?" *Educational Review* 64 (December 1922): 392–94; Frank N. Freeman, "Sorting the Students," *Educational Review* 68 (November 1924): 169–74.

13. Maximilian P. E. Groszmann, "Special and Ungraded Classes," *Journal of Education* 85 (January 26, 1922): 102.

14. Cited in Scheerenberger, *History of Mental Retardation*, 168.

15. Lord, "The Mentally Retarded," 636; Andrew W. Edson, "Exceptional Children in Public Schools," *Journal of Education* 95 (June 1, 1922): 595–96; Osgood, *For "Children Who Vary from the Normal Type*," 135–42; Sarason and Doris, *Educational Handicap*, 308–9.

16. Cited in Sarason and Doris, *Educational Handicap*, 305–6; Special Class Teachers of Boston, *The Boston Way: Plans for the Development of the Individual Child*, 4th ed. (Boston, MA, 1928). See also Osgood, *For "Children Who Vary from the Normal Type*," 142.

17. Harriet Lyman, in *20th Annual Report of the Superintendent of the Boston Public Schools* (1900), appendix 86.

18. Anna M. Kordsiemon, "Construction Work—Its Value in the Subnormal School," *Journal of the National Education Association* 2 (1917): 579.

19. Kordsiemon, "Construction Work," 579.

20. V. V. Anderson, cited in Sarason and Doris, *Educational Handicap*, 312.

21. Wallin, *Education of Handicapped Children*, 249–50.

22. E. R. Johnstone, "The Problem of the Feeble-Minded Child," *Indiana Bulletin* 107 (December 1916): 466.

23. Cited in Osgood, *For "Children Who Vary from the Normal Type*," 143.

24. James G. Riggs, "Training of Teachers for Special Classes," *Journal of the National Education Association* 2 (1917): 881.

25. Dallas D. Johnson, "The Special Child and the Visiting Teacher," *Journal of the National Education Association* 2 (1917): 581.

26. Groszmann, "Special and Ungraded Classes," 102–3.

27. Cited in Osgood, *For "Children Who Vary from the Normal Type*," 132–33;

28. H. E. Blackmar and Anna M. Kordsiemon, "Overcoming the Objection of Parents to the Special Class—Can It Be Done? How?" *Journal of the National Education Association* 3 (1918): 395—98.

29. The *Journal of Exceptional Children* started publishing in 1935 and is a rich resource for information on all aspects of the field. A representative (by no means exhaustive) sample of professional development titles from this era include Bernice Leland, "Case Study Approach to Difficulty in Reading," *Childhood Education* 13 (April 1937): 374–78; Rose S. Hardwick, "Types of Reading Disability," Childhood Education 8 (April 1932): 423–27; Inis B. Hall, "Practical Treatment of the Deaf-Blind," *Journal of Exceptional Children* 3 (April 1937): 102–6; Bernice Elliott, "Learning to Teach Cripples," *Journal of Education* 115 (December 19, 1932): 691–93; Annie Dolman Inskeep, "Help for the Maladjusted Child," *Journal of Education* 120 (May 3, 1937): 217–21; Louise Strachan, "New Ways for Old in the Care of Delicate Children," *Journal of Exceptional Children* 1 (December 1935): 60–66; Edna M. Kugler, "Efficient and Effective Classroom Management," *Journal of Exceptional Children* 2 (June 1936): 128–34, 138; Elisabeth Guthrie, "The Need for Knowing the Whole Child," *Journal of Exceptional Children* 4 (May 1938): 174–79, 183; Frederick L. Patry, "Teaching the Handicapped Child," *Journal of Education* 116 (September 4, 1933): 333–35.

30. Osgood, *For "Children Who Vary from the Normal Type*," 119–21.

31. Olive M. Jones, "Causes of Juvenile Delinquency," *Journal of Education* 96 (October 12, 1922): 351.

32. Osgood, *For "Children Who Vary from the Normal Type*," 123.

33. Davies, *Social Control of the Mentally Deficient*, 138, 144–45.

34. Wallin, *Education of Handicapped Children*, 127.

35. Osgood, For *"Children Who Vary from the Normal Type,"* 118–26.

36. Franklin C. Hoyt, "The Juvenile Court of New York City," *Journal of the National Education Association* 1 (1916): 838–39.

37. Edgar Dubs Shimer, "The Delinquent," *Journal of the National Education Association* 1 (1916): 840.

38. Winzer, *History of Special Education*, 313–32; Wallin, *Education of Handicapped Children*, 118–24; Osgood, For *"Children Who Vary from the Normal Type,"* 93–95, 117.

39. Harry Best, *Deafness and the Deaf in the United States* (New York, 1943), 449.

40. Winzer, *History of Special Education*, 192–97, 317–20; Best, *Deafness and the Deaf*, 445–58, 545–46; Osgood, For *"Children Who Vary from the Normal Type,"* 99–117; John Vickery Van Cleve and Barry Crouch, *A Place of Their Own: Creating the Deaf Community in America* (Washington, DC, 1989), 117–20; E. S. Tillinghast, "The Oral Method of Education of the Deaf," *Journal of the National Education Association* 2 (1917): 572–76. For a measured evaluation of these methods in American institutions and public schools see Edward M. Gallaudet, "Values in the Education of the Deaf," *Educational Review* 4 (June 1892): 16–26.

41. Osgood, For *"Children Who Vary from the Normal Type,"* 104; Best, *Deafness and the Deaf*, 445–48.

42. Imogen B. Palen, "The Hard of Hearing Child in the Public Schools," *Journal of Education* 103 (January 7, 1926): 11–12.

43. Winzer, *History of Special Education*, 331–32; Harry Best, *Blindness and the Blind in the United States* (New York, 1934), 342–46, 122–24; Wallin, *Education of Handicapped Children*, 118–22. For example, the White House Conference on Child Health and Protection listed day school class and "Braille class" attending in a large number of American cities, but did not explain the nature of these categories. Committee on Physically and Mentally Handicapped, *The Handicapped Child* (New York, 1930), 73–74. Also, it should be noted that Chicago was probably alone among major American cities to establish and maintain a single day facility that served children with all levels of vision impairment, including total blindness. That day school opened in 1900.

44. Best, *Blindness and the Blind*, 343–46.

45. Wallin, *Education of Handicapped Children*, 120–21; Gordon Berry, "Saving the Sight of School Children," *Journal of the National Education Association* 1 (1916): 818.

46. Best, *Blindness and the Blind*, 123; Wallin, *Education of Handicapped Children*, 121; quoted in Osgood, For *"Children Who Vary from the Normal Type,"* 158–59.

47. Best, *Blindness and the Blind*, 343.

48. Osgood, For *"Children Who Vary from the Normal Type,"* 160.

49. Wallin, *Education of Handicapped Children*, 121.

50. Miss Lyon, "Speech Improvement in the Chicago Public Schools," *Journal of the National Education Association* 2 (1917): 864; Mrs. Frank A. Reed, "Speech Work in the Detroit Public Schools," *Journal of the National Education Association* 2 (1917): 865; Osgood, For *"Children Who Vary from the Normal Type,"* 163; Wallin, *Education of Handicapped Children*, 124–25. See also Frederick Martin, "The Problem of the Speech Defective," *Journal of Education* 106 (August 29, 1927): 162–63.

51. Lyon, "Speech Improvement in the Chicago Public Schools," 864.

52. Reed, "Speech Work in the Detroit Public Schools," 865; Wallin, *Education of Handicapped Children*, 125.

53. John F. Reigart, "Speech-Correction as a School Problem," *Journal of the National Education Association* 2 (1917): 868–69. See also Vethake E. Mitchell, "Oral Deformities in Their Relation to Defective Speech," *Journal of the National Education Association* 2 (1917): 869.

54. Alma M. Bullowa, "The Need of Speech Work in the High Schools," *Journal of the National Education Association* 2 (1917): 865–68; Wallin, *Education of Handicapped Children*, 126; Osgood, For *"Children Who Vary from the Normal Type,"* 163.

55. Edson, "Exceptional Children," 595–96; Andrew Edson, "Education for the Handicapped," *Journal of Education* 94 (October 20, 1921): 383–84; Osgood, For *"Children Who Vary from the Normal Type,"* 151–57; Caroline L. McHugh, "Boston Has Hospital School," *Journal of Education* 111 (June 16, 1930): 688.

56. Henry S. Curtis, "Salvaging the Crippled Child," *Journal of Education* 111 (April 14, 1930): 417; Edson, "Exceptional Children," 595–96.

57. Curtis, "Salvaging the Crippled Child," 417; Edson, "Exceptional Children," 595; Peter A. Mortenson, "Crippled Children," *Journal of Education* 97 (March 29, 1923): 342.

58. George C. Francis, "Home Teaching for Crippled Children, "*Journal of Education* 111 (June 16, 1930): 689; "Crippled Children," *Journal of Education* 111 (January 27, 1930): 89; Edson, "Education for the Handicapped," 383.

59. Four of the best sources on these developments are Herbert Kliebard, *The Struggle for the American Curriculum 1893–1958* (New York, 1987); Lawrence Cremin, *The Transformation of the School: Progressivism in American Education 1876–1957* (New York, 1964); David Tyack, *The One Best System* (Cambridge, MA, 1974); and William J. Reese, *The Origins of the American High School* (New Haven, CT, 1995).

60. Winzer, *History of Special Education*, 368–71; Tropea, "Bureaucratic Order and Special Children," 46–51.

61. Committee on Physically and Mentally Handicapped, *The Handicapped Child*, 393–438 (quote is from 401).

62. Gladys G. Ide, "Philadelphia's Orthopedic School," *Journal of Education* 120 (June 7, 1937): 274–76; Olga S. Zufelt, "Sheboygan Makes Handicapped Happy," *Journal of Education* 112 (October 27, 1930): 315–16. See also Hilma A. Anderson, "The Smouse Opportunity School," *Journal of Exceptional Children* 4 (February 1938): 110–15.

63. Ida M. Sutherland, "How Los Angeles Takes Care of Her Exceptional Children," *Journal of Exceptional Children* 4 (April 1938): 159–65; Frank Cody, "How Detroit Provides for Its Atypical Children," *Journal of Education* 120 (June 7, 1937): 267–70; Carrie B. Levy, "Milwaukee's Program of Special Education," *Journal of Exceptional Children* 8 (February 1942): 132–43; Edward H. Stullken, Special Education in Chicago," *Journal of Exceptional Children* 1 (December 1935): 73–75; P. M. Watson, "Cleveland's School for Problem Boys," *Journal of Education* 112 (December 15, 1930): 500.

64. Frank M. Rich, "Paterson Educates the Handicapped," *Journal of Education* 112 (October 6, 1930): 232–33.

65. Rich, 233.

66. Mabel Davison, "Dramatizing Uncle Sam's Post Office," *Journal of Exceptional Children* 5 (January 1938): 89–92.

67. Katherine D. Lynch, "Enrichment of the Program for Subnormal Children," *Journal of Exceptional Children* 5 (November 1938): 49–53.

68. Doris E. Carpenter, "A Transportation Project for Retarded Boys," *Journal of Exceptional Children* 4 (December 1937): 56–60, 69.

69. Augusta L. Feiner, "Dramatic Art in Detroit Special Education Classes," *Journal of Exceptional Children* 8 (May 1942): 255.

70. Vesta S. Thompson, "Poetry and the Exceptional Child," *Journal of Exceptional Children* 3 (December 1936): 35.

71. Joseph A. Moore, "Luring the Laggard," *Journal of Education* 121 (May 1938): 166.

72. State of Indiana, *36th Report of the Superintendent of Public Instruction, Being the 14th Biennial Report* (Indianapolis, IN, 1897/1898), 14. For typical comments regarding conditions in rural schools, see State of Indiana, *24th Biennial Report of the State Superintendent of Public Instruction* (Indianapolis, IN, 1907/1908), 109.

73. State of Indiana, "Report of Decatur County Superintendent," *Report of the Superintendent of Public Instruction* (Indianapolis, IN, 1872/1873, 1881/1882).

74. Samuel R. Laycock, "The Education of Exceptional Children in Smaller Cities or Rural Areas," *Journal of Exceptional Children* 2 (May 1935): 16–17.

75. Helen Heffernan, "Meeting the Needs of Exceptional Children in Rural Schools," *Journal of Exceptional Children* 2 (October 1935): 49.

76. Lily Peter, "An Adventure in Educational Democracy," *Peabody Journal of Education* 17 (September 1939): 113–14.

77. Mary Bryan, "As a Beginner Sees It," *Peabody Journal of Education* 16 (May 1939): 371.

78. Sarah Lovelace, "Our Classroom," *Peabody Journal of Education* 16 (May 1939): 373.

79. Anna Louise Draper, "My Beginning Teaching Experiences," *Peabody Journal of Education* 16 (May 1939): 375.

80. Wanda Hitch, "School Teaching as Seen through the Eyes of a Beginning Teacher," *Peabody Journal of Education* 16 (May 1939): 380.

81. Carmel Leon Jett, "My School in the Hills," *Peabody Journal of Education* 16 (May 1939): 385.

82. Heffernan, "Meeting the Needs," 49.

83. Waring James Fitch, "Detecting Handicapped Children in a Small Community," *Journal of Exceptional Children* 9 (April 1943): 210–11; Marcella S. Cohen, "The Visually Handicapped Child in the Rural Community," *Journal of Exceptional Children* 6 (April 1940): 260–63; Heffernan, "Meeting the Needs,"50.

84. For some examples of school life in the later nineteenth and early twentieth centuries in rural America, see Warren Burton, *The District School as It Was By One Who Went to It* (New York, 1928), and Polly Welts Kaufman, ed., *Women Teachers on the Frontier* (New Haven, CT, 1984). An especially amusing and vivid, albeit fictional, account of life in schools in the rural Midwest in the 1800s is Edward Eggleston, *The Hoosier Schoolmaster* (Bloomington, IN, 1984).

The Worlds of Childhood Disability, 1940–1960: Generating Public Awareness

When I don't catch on at once,
People says I'm just a dunce.
I cain't help it 'cause I'm dense
And was borned without much sense.
You-all that is quick and smart
Had an awful big head-start
On we foolish, stupid folks
That you laughs at in your jokes.
If a feller ain't so spry
In his head, though he does try;
If he ain't got enough brains
To come inside when it rains;
Or if he don't know "straight up,"
No more than a cat or pup—
Cain't tell what it's all about—
It don't do no good to shout
At him when he gits things wrong;
That ain't he'pin' him along.
You ain't got no call to sneer
At him 'cause he ain't "all there":
If you wasn't lucky, you
Might be simple-minded, too.

—Mayhew Mantor, 1934

The era from 1940 to 1960 altered the lives of children in the United States in several ways. The legacy of the Depression, the consequences of World War II, and the emergence of new ideas about the nature and health of American society and the American character led to new views about the worlds of children identified as disabled. These twenty years brought a dramatically heightened visibility and awareness of disability to the public, prompting greater scrutiny of the institutions and policies that affected the lives of exceptional children. Through public discussion of the proper role of the disabled in society, in formal school settings, in the family and in the community, disability among children became of greater public concern. In these contexts children with disabilities achieved a higher profile than ever before.

PROFESSIONAL LITERATURE: NEW IDEAS EMERGE

By the late 1930s and 1940s, thanks to over a century of experience with residential institutions and several decades of wrestling with the incorporation of special education in the public schools, those involved in working with children with disabilities had both the background and the opportunity to reflect on that work. These reflections emerged in a limited body of literature by and for educational professionals. Yet observations by educators on the nature and future of special education filtered out into the general public and stimulated more reactions, new perspectives, and calls to action. The public proved especially interested in professional discussions of the nature of individual differences and origins of disability; the proper roles for disabled persons in society and school; and the merits and drawbacks of fully segregated facilities for residential and public school special education.[1]

One of the first articles in this era to express new views on disabled children was written by noted educator Goodwin Watson and published in the March 1938 issue of *Childhood Education*. Watson's essay, titled "The Exceptional Child As a Neglected Resource," issued a provocative challenge to educational professionals and the American public: find ways and means to take advantage of all that disabled children have to offer. Watson's view represented one of the earliest and most blunt challenges to the problem- or deficit-driven paradigm that had long dominated special education and the social treatment of disability.

Watson argued that there existed two distinct worldviews regarding the relation of the individual to society. The first was that "human beings are seen through the appraising eye of an employer in a competitive culture." Accordingly, an employer will judge a person's worth by whether or not he or she is capable of successfully competing against others for a job. "His goal is to select the workers who can produce more efficiently than the others. . . . Only the fit and favored get anywhere. The rest are discards and failures." This staunchly Social Darwinist view contrasted dramatically with the other worldview that "human beings may be viewed not as a means to the most efficient possible production, but as uniquely valuable in themselves. . . . People who are relatively somewhat inferior may yet, in an absolute sense, be very valuable resources." Watson clearly advocated the second view: "We are obligated, it seems to me, to shape a culture which uses the capacities of all our people, whatever their level."[2]

Watson wrote with particular passion about the application of this second worldview to *all* children. "But, can everyone contribute? My answer is an unqualified "Yes,'" he wrote. "I want to apply this same concept whenever a child is added to the two billion inhabitants of the earth. Potentially he is a valuable resource. . . . We are none of us ready to meet certain conceivable standards of social usefulness, but under proper encouragement we can contribute something. So can the exceptional child." Chastising the "snobbery" that "fails to honor all forms of useful work," Watson argued forcefully that virtually any child could contribute to society in some way, through some means. He looked forward to "a time when movies and newspapers will glorify the essential workers rather than, as so often appears, the prosperous parasites." He concluded: "Our society has not yet placed an adequate value upon its human resources. A child is not merely raw material to be fitted as well as the next one into existing social institutions. . . . One valid test of our culture is its ability to create an approved and rewarding place in which every child may serve his fellowmen."[3]

Although other educators may not have agreed with Watson's sharp critique of American society at the time, many did share his belief that it was time society recognized the remarkable potential of children with disabilities. Many of those who called for a new perception of disability subscribed to the concept of "child accounting," that is, "the adjustment of educational offering to the nature and needs of the students." Child accounting, according to one administrator, "would completely revolutionize school buildings, textbooks, methods, marks, and every other aspect of educational behavior. Indeed, revolutionary changes have already taken place because of the tendency toward individualization."[4] Teacher training emphasized individualization much more than it had a generation earlier, and the close link between special education and individualization of instruction caught the attention of many. Margaret A. Neuber, a special educator from Pennsylvania, noted that all persons were "exceptional" in their own way and that historically most work in special education had assumed that "exceptionality" implied a "lack" of something as expressed through a disability label. "Thus, in the very outset," she wrote, "our approach is a limiting one, limiting us and the child and putting down upon him, such a thought as, 'Yes, but, poor dear, he's a cripple.'" Neuber considered such a view of exceptionality damaging and outdated. She suggested "a change of approach from *exception* to *possibility* in any consideration of, or dealings with, the exceptional or atypical child" (emphasis in the original). For Neuber, exceptionality and individuality implied a completeness and a wholeness for a person, not a deficit—a "part of the manifest individuality of the child."[5]

Even before the United States was attacked at Pearl Harbor and entered World War II in December 1941, Americans were concerned about national preparedness in the face of spreading war in Europe and Asia. Such concern led many to rethink notions about the social worth of persons with disabilities in society. Writing just before the United States entered the war, Elise Martens of the U.S. Office of Education expressed her conviction that all members of society could and should be prepared to contribute to the strength of the nation. "There can be no strength and security for America unless there is security for her weakest citizens. . . . An education for exceptional children adjusted to their needs and capacities is an absolutely necessary correlate to an education, for *all* children, that shall make America strong" (emphasis in the original).[6] Martens challenged all teachers in special education to examine their own classrooms and evaluate their own efforts in teaching toward this goal. In defending the idea that special education had an important role in the war effort, Edgar Doll of the Vineland Training School in New Jersey insisted that children with disabilities be treated with dignity: "Far from considering them as social flotsam, the newer attitudes call for respect rather than pity, cooperation rather than patronage, assimilation rather than segregation. . . . Our efforts have been ill spent if the public has not yet learned that the handicapped child is with us, will always be among us, has an important place in the human social family circle, and can hold up his own end if given a chance to do so."[7] Doll then described multiple ways in which such children could contribute to the cause. Another administrator put it simply: "We have come to a time when [a child] is likely to be judged by his *abilities* rather than by his *disabilities*" (emphasis in the original).[8]

Once the war ended in 1945, special educators continued to adjust their assumptions and principles in response to changing social conditions and evolving understandings of disability. One of the most comprehensive analyses to appear in the professional literature came from Harrison Allen Dobbs, a professor of social welfare from Louisiana State University with a strong interest in school children with disabilities. Dobbs published a series of articles over a period of nearly four years during the early 1950s in the *Peabody Journal of Education* that addressed fundamental issues of special education policy and practice. While much of what Dobbs had to say related to social agencies, community activities, and families, he also addressed fundamental issues of changing assumptions and perceptions related to disability and special education that had been raised prior to and during World War II.

Dobbs' central premise was that children with "defects" were not necessarily "handicapped," and that multiple approaches and resources—carefully conceived, coordinated, and executed—could truly alter the ways in which society viewed disability and disabled children. Dobbs articulated several principles in his series of articles, most notably that "all children, whatever their characteristics, should command society's fullest respect and aid." His view that all children could contribute to society and did not necessarily deserve a negative label such as "handicapped" built on similar expressions from the two previous decades. As a social welfare advocate, Dobbs suggested that families should work with family support services as well as schools to effect changes and strategies suggested by research and experience. As a scholar, he called on a variety of academic disciplines including sociology, psychology, education, medicine, public administration, and social work to dedicate research and field work to providing support for families and children beset with "defect." He urged academics to ask questions, survey existing conditions and practices, and make recommendations for changes and improvements in services. His final article, published in 1953, called for a "dynamic and experimental, not static" approach to addressing these issues. This approach included working for an appropriate education for exceptional children based on living a "full, changing" life; emphasizing preventive rather than curative approaches; accenting the "positive rather than the negative" aspects of disabled children; and coordinating localized efforts to assist such children. All such efforts, he stated, would "help advance American child welfare, *children with defects particularly*" (emphasis in the original).[9]

The assumption that a child with an identified disability was a significant social and educational liability disturbed others as well as Dobbs. Ivan Garrison, director of special education in the Jacksonville, Illinois, public schools, called for "a broader concept of normalcy" that recognized the value and dignity of all differences among children, regardless of their origin or nature. Garrison maintained that then-current conceptions of *normalcy* were too limiting and were being confused with *average*. "Both terms are really more applicable to statistics than they are to human beings," he claimed. "We all (and I don't mean just specialists) must help in freeing society of its *overgrown fear of deviations from its fortuitous standards of normalcy*" (emphasis in the original). The separation of significant disability from a place along a continuum of individual differences, he argued, only served to absolve everyone but special educators of working for the benefit of disabled children. In fact, he said, exceptional children were "in many areas . . . closer to normalcy than they are to the extremes." Such statements of principle emphasizing the positive attributes of children with disabilities and the need to see their possibilities rather than their deficits continued to appear in journals throughout the 1950s.[10]

SPECIAL EDUCATION IN THE PUBLIC SCHOOLS: LIMITED CHANGE

Even as new theories and assumptions regarding disability and special education generated energetic discussion in the professional literature, traditional views of disabled children and special education became further entrenched in the public schools of the United States. Although some in the field openly questioned the propriety and effectiveness of segregated settings for students with disabilities, the near-universal practice was to establish and maintain separate classes, schools, and programs that permitted little if any contact between special education students and their nondisabled peers. The belief persisted that the special nature of the curriculum and instruction for special education students mandated segregated settings and that *all* students benefited from this separation. Children with disabilities, it was argued, received more appropriate instruction and closer attention in such settings. Meanwhile their "normal" peers in regular classrooms could proceed through the school curriculum without being slowed down or "burdened" by overly needy learners demanding too much of the teacher's time and attention.[11]

Within schools, special education changed only slightly between 1940 and 1960. Descriptions of "best practices" in the classroom continued to feature advances in strategies for curriculum and instruction. The continued extension of special education into secondary education—junior and senior high schools and comparable segregated settings for students with disabilities—paralleled the rapidly expanding availability and reach of secondary schooling across the country and garnered particular attention. Furthermore, a heightened interest in the "nonacademic" or social aspects of special education emerged as the issue of effective social adjustment of students with disabilities—especially those identified as "juvenile delinquents"—within society and beyond school attracted greater concern in the postwar era.

Within the thousands of special education settings spread throughout the United States, there was some change among some of the relatively new providers: public and private nursery schools. Responding to calls for earlier identification of and interventions for children with disabilities, schooling before first grade assumed a key role in finding children with disabilities and getting them started on their special education in order to better prepare them for the traditional grades. For example, a private nursery school in Minnesota intentionally enrolled children who were blind, deaf, and mentally disabled in order to enrich the social experiences of the many students in the school who were of normal or above-normal intelligence. "Our experience has convinced us that an occasional atypical child can be absorbed into a nursery school group with actual benefit to all concerned," reported one of the teachers. "They can be taught that it is not charity but a privilege when they sometimes help a deaf Sally or a blind Patty or a dull Tom."[12] Another nursery school in California offered a detailed analysis of the ways in which "Jack," a three-year-old with multiple disabilities, benefited from his attendance and participation in the program.[13]

For the regular grades of public school, however, the focus continued on delivering a specialized program in a segregated setting. The arts continued as a favored area of instruction for students with all kinds of disabilities. Puppet shows, music (singing, percussion, and instrument playing), drama and theater, dancing, painting, construction projects, and clay modeling were particular favorites for children with physical and/or cognitive disabilities. Teachers who used these approaches asserted that the arts generated great enjoyment and enthusiasm among their pupils and helped them develop cooperative social skills. In a Philadelphia school for children with physical disabilities, students such as Mary ("a sharp-tongued, asocial child"); Joan (a "spastic" girl who loved music); Frank (a "cripple" with braced legs); and Betty ("a sulky, bad-tempered little girl that hated the world") apparently underwent significant positive personality changes when given the opportunity to express themselves artistically.[14] A school in Detroit for "backward" children found that the use of art could unlock the confidence of children who had not profited by earlier school experiences. Teachers argued that students in special classes for "retarded" children that provided a reasonable pace for academic study, complemented by artistic endeavors of all kinds, found their school experiences to be much more tolerable and successful.[15]

Even as interest in teaching special education using the arts grew, so did concern about socializing disabled children and helping them develop a more authentic understanding of their physical and social environments. Public school educators became especially interested in "crippled" children and those with modality deficits (deafness and/or blindness), although they were a very small percentage of all students in special education.

Children who were blind, for example, required more effective efforts to help them understand scale and proportion in their interpretation of the physical world. As a result, many blind children engaged in model making, map making, and written activities related to processing their experiences in creating these objects. Others argued that blind children needed more extensive socialization activities to help overcome family and societal prejudices about their condition. Games and activities that would help "normal" persons—adults and children—understand what it was like to be blind and that would give the blind child a sense of stability and acceptance became popular components of her or his education. "Blindness is certainly a handicap to an individual," wrote Virginia Axline of Columbia University, "but the lack of acceptance of themselves as individuals is a greater handicap than the blindness."[16] A similar case was made for children who were partially or totally deaf. Margaret Radcliffe, director of the San Diego Society for the Hard of Hearing, used virtually identical language: "The hard of hearing child in our schools is handicapped more by a lack of *understanding* of his problem on the part of his parents, teachers and friends than by his impaired hearing" (emphasis in the original). Socialization skills and the emotional state of physically disabled children thus assumed primary importance in considerations for their proper, special education.[17]

In line with progressive ideas regarding the importance of "life adjustment" to the school curriculum and amid the long tradition of concern about juvenile delinquency, public schools targeted students with behavioral problems early on in their education. Many professional journals for educators included case studies of such students. For example, an article in *Childhood Education* profiled five-year-old "Daniel," who was a chronically ill child who panicked when in a school classroom and held a deeply abnormal attachment to his mother. He "showed low average general intelligence" and "was immature in his speech, vocabulary, ability to handle materials and to draw." The article traced Daniel's family history and described how intervention, first by a competent psychologist and then by a caring teacher, helped him adjust to school life.[18]

Another boy, eight-year-old "Wendell," was a highly intelligent child exhibiting what today likely would be labeled Attention Deficit–Hyperactivity Disorder (ADHD). "He seemed to react to every stimulus at one and the same time. He darted, he pounced, he fell, he skated, he ran—he was never seen to walk.... He poked, he pushed, he bopped children whenever and wherever he passed them—and all of this seemingly without rancor, without malice but with merriment in his eyes and a laugh on his lips." Despite mixed feelings for Wendell at his school, after one year under careful and caring tutelage, Wendell had become much more manageable.[19] Another example came from Charlotte Kwiat, who described her first year of teaching in a Chicago classroom in an impoverished neighborhood that was commonly called "Little Hell." Her descriptions of the behavior of her students were vivid: "a classroom . . . not unlike a three-ring circus . . . Boys swung from ceiling lights, erasers were being tossed . . . girls with high heels and painted faces were laughing raucously. . . . However, I wasn't licked." Kwiat described how through patience and empathy she gained control of the students. Such case studies aimed to provide both comfort and hope to teachers and parents coping with similar situations.[20]

Identifying children exhibiting or holding the potential for significant behavioral or emotional disorders required skilled observation by and interaction among teachers, families, and school professionals. Distinguishing between normal childhood misbehavior and serious emotional maladjustment proved as difficult as it was important. In such determinations, teachers learned to focus on two key concepts, "personality" and "emotional adjustment," and to pay attention to the consistency and intensity of the behavior as well as to look for aggressive and/or "retiring" behavior. Teachers were also advised to look for certain excessive physical behaviors such as nail-biting, twitchings, chewing, hair-twisting, or scratching. Other factors indicating potential disorders included below-average intelligence, poverty, and—especially in the case of girls—"oversexuality." In addition to recognizing such disorders, teachers tried to determine the reasons for the problem and then refer serious cases to the school psychologist. Debate swirled as to the role of home life and parenting actions in developing emotional or behavioral disorders, especially

"delinquency." A common assumption was that the home was certainly significant and possibly could partner effectively with schools and social agencies
in prevention, detection, and correction.[21]

Experts viewed delinquency and emotional "maladjustment" as especially
problematic by the time a student reached high school, when she or he was that
much closer to leaving school and assuming an adult role in society. In fact,
the school experience and vocational preparation for all high school students
with disabilities—not just those with behavioral or emotional disorders—
constituted a matter of considerable urgency for school professionals and
special educators. Writing in 1941, a school psychologist from Butte, Montana,
lamented how many high schools failed all too often to provide appropriate
services for "slow-learning" pupils. Teachers assumed such students just didn't
"belong," especially if a school district hadn't yet found the resources or the
desire to provide high quality special education. She noted about the students,
"You know them. They are unhappy, misplaced, thwarted, and baffled. They
form a fine audience for crack brains and demagogues. They do not fit into the
social structure of the school, and are there only because there is no other place
for them."[22] Her comments could not be applied universally, because many
large public school systems had included special education in high schools
since at least the 1920s. Nevertheless, in less populous regions with limited
resources and even more limited traditions of high school attendance, many
educators considered high school a different world that was less suited to
children with disabilities.

Consequently, over the next two decades efforts intensified to bring special
education more effectively to the high school. Because so much of secondary
education still focused on preparation for work and citizenship—only a minority of students continued on a college preparation track—the development of
functional social and vocational skills took center stage. Developing adequate
socialization skills consisted of a multifaceted approach: providing academic
instruction that "should be bent to giving as good an education as [a student]
can take"; adjusting instruction so that the student felt an authentic sense of
achievement and accomplishment; relating that work directly and vividly to
a student's life both in and outside of school; offering direct instruction in
various social skills such as accepting unpleasant but unavoidable events as
normal; and improving other skills such as functional reading and good work
habits.[23] At the heart of a stable and successful social life for adolescents, argued educational psychologist Samuel Laycock, stood three features: "getting
a sane view of oneself," "understanding the behavior of one's fellows," and

"adjusting to the Infinite," the last referring to a sense of spirituality and an awareness of humankind's place in the Universe. While the last point may have seemed impossibly abstract for most adolescents with disabilities, a decent sense of self-esteem and the ability to interact with others clearly stood out as prerequisites for a successful life beyond the high school. Such development thus emerged as an important expectation of secondary special education.[24]

By the mid-1950s, public schools in most areas of the country paid attention to and provided for, at least to some extent, children with a variety of disabilities. Nationally, special educators and school administrators constantly noted that the number of students with disabilities formally identified and served in public schools was far below the actual number of such children enrolled, and that most schools failed to provide adequately for every child who required special education. Estimates for the actual number of children with disabilities always dramatically exceeded the number formally identified as such. This combination of incomplete identification and insufficient provision of educational services alarmed the growing number of parents, teachers, administrators, and other professionals involved in the field. Despite the structures in place, most professionals still claimed that the public schools of the United States inadequately provided for disabled children. Consequently, other settings—especially the residential institutions—were called on to help contribute more fully to special education. Moreover, advocacy groups and other citizens familiar with disability and its impact on families and society sought to raise the profile of disability and those affected by it.

LIFE IN RESIDENTIAL INSTITUTIONS: ALARMING REVELATIONS

Even as public schools took on a far greater number and percentage of children identified as disabled, residential institutions for persons with disabilities continued to play an important role in public policy regarding disability. That role, however, experienced an increasing level of attention and criticism throughout the 1940s and 1950s as the institutions grew tremendously in size, altered significantly the nature of their residential populations, and fell under the intense and often unforgiving scrutiny of an increasingly attentive and concerned public. In particular, a series of photographic and narrative essays on the living conditions for those housed in residential institutions—especially those for the mentally disabled—provided shocking evidence that many if not most such places offered nothing but hellish, brutal worlds for those entrusted to their care.

Between 1940 and 1960, residential institutions for the disabled continued down a familiar path. They remained overcrowded while maintaining long waiting lists for admission. They had various combinations of educational, social, vocational, and custodial purposes. In institutions for the mentally disabled, custodial care was the chief method for organizing the lives of residents. Parents or guardians experienced more and more pressure from doctors, social workers, and public school personnel to place seriously disabled children in an institution, to "put them away" in order to ease the burden and stigma on other family members. By the early 1960s, there existed 738 public and private residential institutions serving nearly 112,000 children and adults in the United States who were disabled by deafness, blindness, mental retardation, and/or emotional disorders.[25]

Superintendents of residential institutions had always carefully crafted the public image of their facilities to reflect modern, scientific approaches to education and treatment in caring and productive environments. Much of their success in maintaining a positive public image arose from highly limited and carefully screened accessibility to life within their walls. Administrators typically admitted only visitors who were sympathetic with the mission and method of the facility and who would report accordingly. Staff carefully limited and controlled parents' contact with their children inside the institution. Public perception of life inside such institutions thus relied heavily on what superintendents said and promised. By the mid-1900s, however, an increasing number of observers and visitors gained access to institutions who previously had no interest or reason to do so. What they found proved shocking and disheartening. Although external agencies such as the American Association of Mental Deficiency had begun to develop formal standards to measure the quality of such institutions, their rapid growth, astonishingly high staff turnover rates of poorly trained personnel, and inadequate funding and space led to a significant and widespread deterioration of their facilities and services.

Photographic essays and narrative commentaries placed the institutions under a harsh and disturbing public microscope, particularly during the 1940s. Perhaps the most notable of these were three separate series of photograph essays taken at different times of New York's Letchworth Village, a residential facility for persons with mental disabilities that had a national reputation as an exemplar of sound and humane practices. Comparing these three separate projects demonstrated the power of photography not only to convey various "realities" but also to shape public opinion. The first, a series of staged images and posed portraits of uniformed inmates (then called "patients") by Margaret Bourke-White taken in the early 1930s, showed an organized, clean, humane facility full of useful activity. In 1941, however, photographer Arnold Genthe published a much different series of photographic images of Letchworth, showing inmates "as workers" with little to suggest, noted historian James Trent, "a world outside the institution. Genthe's patients were peasant-like, rooted in a community . . . they were not likely to leave."[26]

The third series appeared in 1948. Taken by photographer Irving Haberman, these photographs constituted an actual exposé of the institution, depicting "wretched conditions. . . . Naked residents, unkempt and dirty, huddled in sterile dayrooms. Haberman's patients were helpless quasi-human beings."[27] The photographs appeared in Albert Deutsch's volume *The Shame of the States*, a harsh critique of conditions found mostly in hospitals for the mentally ill but that also included a blunt condemnation of Letchworth Village. Noting that Letchworth Village was "one of America's most famous institutions for the feeble-minded," Deutsch stated bluntly that the institution "suffers acutely from the twin diseases that afflict most state institutions for the mentally handicapped—overcrowding and understaffing. These twin evils carry in their train a long line of deficiencies." Deutsch also protested the lack of scientific research at the facility as well as New York State's unwillingness to fund it to even a minimally acceptable level.[28]

In addition to photographic representations, narratives describing conditions at several institutions for the mentally disabled appeared during and after the Second World War. Men classified as Conscientious Objectors during World War II often served alternative obligations in residential institutions for the disabled. Such individuals kept detailed records and diaries describing their experiences and the conditions within such institutions. They consistently documented wretched conditions, patient neglect, inadequate numbers of poorly trained staff, and repeated patterns of violence and abuse against the "residents." The lack of adequate funding often led to using high-grade inmates as "staff," a situation that led to further degrading treatment and horrific conditions. Newspaper reporters often followed up the publication of these reports with their own eyewitness descriptions. Although resisted by some of the superintendents, these reports, according to James Trent, "were too consistent and too numerous to dismiss."[29]

Commentary from the residents themselves, although rare and almost never published while they were institutionalized, verified such negative depictions of life in the institutions. In his 2004 book, *The State Boys Rebellion*, journalist and author Michael D'Antonio gave voice to several individuals who were committed to the Walter E. Fernald State School near Boston during the 1940s. D'Antonio's account of life in the institution during the 1940s and 1950s validated the widespread negative descriptions of the time: the poorly trained, often abusive, staff; the lack of sufficient funding; the aging and inadequate space and facilities; and the abandonment as well as neglect of needy and deserving children by family and friends. One boy, Bobby Williams, recalled decades after the fact that James McGinn, one of the attendants, "did things in a way that you knew what was coming. I think that's why some kids pushed him more. They felt like they could tell when to stop before he hurt them. But that didn't always happen, and the stuff he did made you feel really bad." Freddy Boyce, the central protagonist in the book, reflected that "I could see the attendants were overwhelmed, and a lot of them weren't that smart, or patient, to start with. When things were bad, the noise in the ward could be deafening, with all these kids talking and making noise. It was a real cacophony. And a lot of the time, one attendant would have to handle a ward alone, or two wards. It was practically impossible. They would lose it." Another boy named Joey, who helped maintain the school human specimen laboratory, recalled that the attendants used to warn him that if he didn't behave he would "wind up in one of Dr. Benda's pickle jars." In the 1970s, when several of the residents successfully sued the state after they had been given Thorazine and other experimental drugs without their knowledge or permission through "The Science Club" in the 1950s, Larry Nutt commented on both his life at Fernald and the entire system of the treatment of the mentally disabled. That system "ruined my life," he said. "I don't believe we know all the stuff they did to us. I don't know if we will ever know the whole truth." The exposés and commentary from the 1960s and 1970s strongly suggest that such conditions and complaints changed little over the next twenty years.[30]

CONFESSIONAL LITERATURE AND ADVOCACY GROUPS: GENERATING PUBLIC SYMPATHY

The recognition of the presence of persons with disabilities in society gained significant ground from 1940 to 1960. The solidifying role of public schools in special education, the increasing populations of persons in residential facilities for the disabled, and the growing attention to the relation among families, social services, and disability all promoted attention toward the disabled. The impact of World War II had a dramatic and fundamental affect on social perceptions of disability. With disabled persons filling in satisfactorily in jobs formerly held by men who joined the armed forces, and with the return of tens of thousands of disabled veterans to work and to educational institutions, public awareness of disability became generally more positive and accepting. Even so, declaring or confessing to having a child with a disability remained extremely difficult for many owing to the social stigma still attached to hereditary notions about various disabilities. Moreover, professionals frequently advised parents to institutionalize disabled children—especially those with serious intervention needs. To address such concerns, some celebrities took it upon themselves to educate the public about the presence as well as positive aspects of disabled children in society. Furthermore, groups of interested parties joined together in official organizations to advance the cause of their loved ones with disabilities.

A variety of narratives that described the challenges and joys of having a disabled child in a family appeared in magazines and other formats during the late 1940s and early 1950s. One of the most noted and widely read came from a well-known author. In 1950, Pearl Buck, author of the immensely popular book *The Good Earth* and other well-known stories, published a series of articles in the *Ladies' Home Journal* entitled "The Child Who Never Grew"; it appeared in book form soon thereafter. In this narrative, Buck described the struggles of parenting and coping with a child with severe mental retardation—her daughter Carol. Buck acknowledged the tremendous "sorrow" she encountered upon learning of Carol's disability and the difficulty of coming to terms with the fact that her dreams for her child would never come to pass. Buck's skills as a writer were evident as she explored the process by which she came to understand her daughter was disabled and her experiences in trying to ascertain the best course of action for her care. She detailed her waxing and waning sensibilities of despair, joy, optimism, resignation, confusion, and anger as she negotiated the difficult path of parenting well while dealing with ignorance, skepticism, and patronization on the part of family, friends, and professionals. Hers was a remarkably honest yet tender statement that accurately reflected social attitudes toward disability at the time.[31]

Buck saw the book as a means to fulfill a clear mission: to help society understand what trials and strengths a disabled child can bring to a family. Noting that the time had come to tell Carol's story, Buck wrote that "there is afoot in our country a great new movement to help all children like her. . . . We

are beginning to understand the importance and the significance of the mentally retarded person in our human society. . . . The old stigma of 'something
in the family' is all too often unjust." She cautioned that mental disability "is
enough to cause trouble everywhere. Homes are unhappy, parents distraught,
schoolrooms confused by the presence of these who for no fault of their own
are as they are. . . . And all they do is done in innocence, for of God's many
children these are the most innocent."[32]

Her primary task as a parent, as she saw it, was to accept the inevitable.
A doctor at the Mayo Clinic in Minnesota did his best to help her understand:

> "Listen to what I tell you!" he commanded. "I tell you, madame,
> the child can never be normal. Do not deceive yourself. You will
> wear out your life and beggar your family unless you give up hope
> and face the truth. . . . Americans are all too soft. I am not soft. It is
> better to be hard, so that you can know what to do. This child will be
> a burden on you all your life. . . . Prepare yourself, madame! Above
> all, do not let her absorb you. Find a place where she can be happy
> and leave her there and live your own life. I tell you the truth for
> your own sake." . . . I shall forever be grateful to him, whose name
> I do not even know. He cut the wound deep, but it was clean and
> quick. I was brought at once face to face with the inevitable.

Her narrative continued with details regarding her visits to other doctors, to
schools and institutions, and her eventual coming to terms with her situation and her eventual decision to institutionalize Carol. Buck recognized the
struggles involved but insisted that well-trained professionals and continued
research could dramatically improve the lot of such children and their families. "Hope brings comfort," she concluded. "What has been need not forever
continue to be so. It is too late for some of our children, but if their plight
can make people realize how unnecessary much of the tragedy is, their lives,
thwarted as they are, will not have been meaningless. Again, I speak as one
who knows."[33]

Buck's direct, honest, and deeply personal testimony struck a chord with
innumerable readers. So did another brief chronicle by a famous mother
confronting her child's disability. *Angel Unaware* was published in 1953 by
noted personality Dale Evans Rogers, wife and performing partner of the
famous actor-singer Roy Rogers and an immensely popular figure in her
own right during the early 1950s. Rogers wrote the book from the narrative

perspective of her infant daughter, Robin, who was born with Down syndrome, a damaged heart, and other multiple complications and who passed away two days before her second birthday. In the book, Robin speaks to God about her time "Down There," representing the Rogerses' strong belief that her life and disabilities reflected God's "Plan" to teach humans about love, compassion, patience, and faith. The book is filled with references to the Rogerses' devout Christianity. Rogers wrote in the foreword that her daughter "came into the world with an appalling handicap" but that she and her husband "learned some great lessons of truth through His tiny messenger."[34]

While the book by design was heavily couched in a childlike innocence and optimism, it nonetheless addressed important issues of families affected by disability. At the outset of the book, Rogers has Robin describe her birth and the cool, distant professional concern of her doctors. Robin says that it was days before they informed Mrs. Rogers of Robin's condition because "they were all dreading the time when they'd have to tell Mommy and Daddy about the bad shape I was in. . . . That's one thing I learned Down There . . . that the doctors are just beginning to discover how much help You [God] are in any situation. They're beginning to talk seriously about 'tender, loving care.' You are getting through to the doctors." Rogers described through Robin's perspective the daily struggles of feeding and the constant suggestions that she be put away: "it was easier to do it quickly, before the child became entrenched in their hearts. . . . Daddy said, 'No! We'll keep her and do all we can for her, and take our chances." The book continued to detail the heartache and sense of guilt felt by Roy and Dale when they went to work and had to leave Robin with nurses. As did many parents, the Rogers sought out specialists and looked for a miracle cure. But they also realized that God's Plan may well involve Robin's early death. In a stunning passage, the child asked for God's forgiveness for a doctor who "said that babies who came into the world in my condition should be lined up in a row and 'machine-gunned,' because they were no good to themselves or to anybody else." After Robin's death, the Rogers family committed itself to advocating on behalf of all children with disabilities. In the book, referring to her parents, Robin says, "They're a lot stronger, since they got Our message."[35]

Rogers' book literally angelicized children with disabilities, offering a stark and potent contrast to views of disabled children as dark, bedeviled, cursed, or delinquent. Both Dale Rogers and Pearl Buck helped families of disabled children—especially parents—understand that they were not alone in their struggles, guilt, shame, or confusion.

In fact, well before either book was published, parents had sought ways to support each other in efforts to make their lives and those of their disabled children richer and more dignified. Informal groups formed in various states in the late 1930s and by the early 1950s had coalesced into formal associations. While professional associations of doctors, educators, and other professionals had formed in the 1800s around categories of disability—associations for the deaf, the blind, and the mentally disabled led the way—associations formed for parents and other advocates addressed purposes more social and political than scholarly or professional. The National Association of Parents and Friends of Retarded Children, the most high-profile of these, arose through the consolidated efforts of local advocacy groups and gained formal status in 1950. Between 1950 and 1980 the association changed its name and image several times, from the original name to the National Association for Retarded Children, the National Association for Retarded Citizens, and finally to its current name, The Arc. Eventually this organization would inspire other advocates for children with specific disabilities to form as well, bringing a much stronger voice to and for children with disabilities. By the 1960s and 1970s such groups, especially The Arc, had become major players in shaping and improving the lives of disabled children. The following chapter will examine how the National Association of Parents and Friends of Retarded Children, other organizations, the federal government, along with changing views of special education produced dramatic developments that affected the lives of children with disabilities between 1960 and 1980.[36]

NOTES

1. An excellent and concise example of such a call to reflection is Elise H. Martens, "Education for a Strong America," *Journal of Exceptional Children* 8 (November 1941): 36–41.

2. Goodwin Watson, "The Exceptional Child As a Neglected Resource," *Childhood Education* 14 (March 1938): 296–97.

3. Ibid., 297–99. *Educational Forum* 7 (January 1943): 157.

4. Andrew W. Hunt, "Child Accounting—Its Value From a Pedagogical and Administrative Standpoint," *Educational Forum* 7 (January 1943): 157.

5. Margaret A. Neuber, "Believe It—Or Not," *Journal of Exceptional Children* 7 (November 1940): 48–50.

6. Martens, "Education for a Strong America," 36, 39–41.

7. Edgar A. Doll, "The Exceptional Child in War Time," *Journal of Exceptional Children* 8 (April 1942): 204–5.

8. Watson B. Miller, "Education and the War," *Journal of Exceptional Children* 9 (May 1943): 237.

9. Harrison Allen Dobbs, "Children with Defects: A Frame of Reference," *Peabody Journal of Education* 27 (January 1950): 228–36; Harrison Allen Dobbs, "Children with Defects: Steps Forward," *Peabody Journal of Education* 29 (November 1951): 157–65; Harrison Allen Dobbs, "More Certainty in Educating Children with Defects," *Peabody Journal of Education* 30 (September 1952): 66–74; Harrison Allen Dobbs, "Children with Defects: A Philosophical Proposal," *Peabody Journal of Education* 31 (September 1953): 67–77.

10. Ivan K. Garrison, "A Broader Concept of Normalcy," *Journal of Education* 136 (March 1954): 178–81.

11. For a more thorough discussion of the debate regarding the segregation of special education students in the 1940s and 1950s, see Robert L. Osgood, *The History of Inclusion in the United States* (Washington, DC, 2005), 42–54.

12. Josephine C. Foster and Marion L. Mattson, "The Atypical Child in an Average School," *Childhood Education* 17 (November 1940): 124.

13. Gladys Gardner, "The Nursery School Helps a Retarded Child," *Childhood Education* 21 (May 1945): 453–56.

14. Georgiana S. Mendenhall, "The Influence of the Arts on the Lives of Handicapped Children," *Journal of Exceptional Children* 7 (October 1940): 11–18, 33–34.

15. Marjorie B. Hicks, "Teaching Art to Backward Children," *Journal of Exceptional Children* 6 (February 1940): 172–75; Louise Laird, "Teaching a Retarded Group," *Journal of Education* 121 (October 1938): 227–28; Lydia A. Duggins, "Exceptional Children in the Classroom," *Journal of Education* 133 (October 1950): 200–2.

16. O. J. Hill, "Another Beam of Light through the Darkness," *Journal of Exceptional Children* 6 (January 1940): 129–37; Irene Marquis, "Helping the Visually Handicapped," *Journal of Education* 134 (March, April, 1951): 106–7; Virginia M. Axline, "Understanding and Accepting the Child Who Is Blind," *Childhood Education* 30 (May 1954): 427–30.

17. Margaret Williams Radcliffe, "The Hard of Hearing Child in Our Schools," *Childhood Education* 21 (May 1945): 457; Duggins, "Exceptional Children in the Classroom," 201. See also Marjorie P. Sheldon, "Protection of the Crippled Child from Avoidable Strain in School," *Journal of Exceptional Children* 8 (November 1940): 50–56; George Lavos, "Personality and a Physical Defect," *Journal of Exceptional Children* 7 (January 1941): 124–28, 145–46.

18. Henry Hansburg, "The Case of Daniel," *Childhood Education* 22 (September 1945): 37–40.

19. Marion Nesbitt, " . . . When the 'Different' Child Is Accepted," *Childhood Education* 27 (January 1951): 218–19.

20. Charlotte Kwiat, "Teaching In Little Hell," *Journal of Education* 133 (December 1950): 258–59.

21. Walter B. Barbe, "Locating Children With Emotional Problems," *Childhood Education* 30 (November 1953): 127–30; M. LaVinia Warner, "Problems of the Delinquent Girl," *Journal of Exceptional Children* 7 (December 1940): 102–7, 112; P. F. Valentine, "They Blame the Home for Delinquency," *Educational Forum* 11 (March 1947): 285–87; Katharine F. Lenroot, "Delinquency Prevention Through School and Social Agency Coordination," *Educational Forum* 8 (November 1943): 11–15. See also Alma May Stewart, "Personnel Work With the Special School Pupil," *Journal of Exceptional Children* 6 (May 1940): 283–87, 306, for an interesting discussion of how a special school's entire staff involved itself in diagnosis and treatment of boys with behavior disorders in Chicago.

22. Catherine Nutterville, "Equality of Educational Opportunity for the Slow-Learning Pupils in High School," *Journal of Exceptional Children* 7 (January 1941): 134.

23. Mabel R. Farson, "Education of the Handicapped Child for Social Competency," *Journal of Exceptional Children* 6 (January 1940): 138–44, 150;

24. Samuel R. Laycock, "Problems in the Adolescence of Exceptional Children," *Journal of Exceptional Children* 9 (April 1943): 203–7.

25. R.C. Scheerenberger, *A History of Mental Retardation* (Baltimore, 1983): 240–41; Romaine Mackie, *Special Education in the United States: Statistics 1948-1966* (New York, 1969), 41.

26. James Trent Jr., *Inventing the "Feeble Mind": A History of Mental Retardation in the United States* (Berkeley, CA, 1994), 225–26.

27. Trent, *Inventing the "Feeble Mind,"* 226–27.

28. Albert Deutsch, *The Shame of the States* (New York, 1948), 132–34.

29. Trent, *Inventing the "Feeble Mind,"* 227–30.

30. Michael D'Antonio, *The State Boys Rebellion* (New York, 2004), 45, 48, 104, 277.

31. Pearl Buck, *The Child Who Never Grew* (New York, 1950).

32. Buck, *The Child Who Never Grew,* 7.

33. Buck, *The Child Who Never Grew,* 22–23, 61–62.

34. Dale Evans Rogers, *Angel Unaware* (Westwood, NJ, 1953), 7.

35. Rogers, *Angel Unaware,* 11–16, 19, 52, 63.

36. Osgood, *The History of Inclusion in the United States,* 56–59.

5

Ensuring the Rights and Enhancing the Lives of Children with Disabilities in and out of the Classroom, 1960–1980

A child with disabilities born in the United States in 1960 came into a nation that was finally claiming to have a significant interest in her or his welfare. Nevertheless, American society struggled to define appropriate services, policies, and practices intended to support the child's education, health, and general well-being. Those struggles intensified between 1960 and 1980. This was an era defined by widespread, urgent, and often painful efforts to realize and safeguard the rights of persons previously marginalized because of race, gender, ethnicity, and other crucial characteristics. The characteristic of disability was no different. Swept up in and contributing to the civil rights movement and other intentional efforts designed to improve the lives of millions, persons with disabilities and their advocates engaged in political, social, and educational initiatives that would challenge and change longstanding policies and practices. As a consequence, there was a profound difference in the anticipated quality of life for a child with disabilities born in 1980 compared to that for her or his counterpart born two decades earlier.

Changes occurred in multiple arenas. The federal government dramatically increased its attention and the amount of its resources devoted to disability. Court decisions and legislation—state as well as federal—fundamentally altered the expectations for public and private agencies to address disability and enhance the lives of those labeled disabled. For the nation's disabled children, the school and other public facilities became, at least in theory, more responsive to their needs and interests. The definition of disability itself underwent significant change. Medical, psychological, and educational professionals examined disabling conditions and created new categories of disability while redefining or even eliminating older ones. The remarkable rise of advocacy for disabled persons, including children, led to a heightened activism on the part of associations for the disabled as well as to the widespread efforts known as the Disability Rights Movement. Even so, the extent to which the actual lives of children with disability changed as a result of these dramatic developments was and continues to be the subject of serious debate. Indeed, the voices of the disabled as well as those of their advocates and their skeptics tell a complicated story.

THE FEDERAL GOVERNMENT AND DISABILITY

The federal government to some extent had been involved in issues related to disability for decades, such as the White House Conferences on Children and Youth (held every ten years) and legislation from the Truman and Eisenhower years addressing employment and training of the disabled and their teachers. Even so, the election of President John F. Kennedy in 1960 marked the beginning of a watershed era for government involvement in the lives of children with disabilities. Certainly, Kennedy's personal interest in disability stemmed to a large extent from his love for his sister Rosemary, who was born with mental retardation. However, the Kennedy administration also worked to advance the rights of many minority groups in the volatile early 1960s, and the disabled represented a logical beneficiary of such efforts. The Joseph P. Kennedy, Jr., Foundation provided strong and generous financial support for efforts to combat mental retardation. Kennedy himself developed a personal relationship with the leadership of the National Association for Retarded Children (NARC), the respected mainstream advocacy group for persons with cognitive disabilities and their families.[1]

Although Kennedy served as president for a relatively short time, his administration engaged in several significant initiatives designed to enhance the lives of the disabled—especially children. In 1961, Kennedy appointed a President's Panel on Mental Retardation. The panel issued a report the following year entitled *A Proposed Program for National Action to Combat Mental Retardation*. The report "constituted a major milestone in the history of mental retardation in the United States" and advocated federal involvement in setting goals, planning services, and funding research and development projects in a range of areas. In 1963, Kennedy organized a White House Panel on Mental Retardation and formed a Division of Handicapped Children and Youth, attached to the U.S. Office of Education and headed by noted special educator Samuel Kirk.[2]

Kennedy's efforts also included the acceleration of federal legislation on behalf of children with disabilities. Following Kennedy's special message to Congress on February 5, 1963, proposing such legislation, two significant laws were passed. PL 88-156 supported state efforts to engage in planning for mental retardation; PL 88-164 designated federal funding for research and construction projects related to special education and other initiatives on behalf of the disabled. After Kennedy's assassination in November 1963, the Johnson Administration continued such efforts as part of Johnson's dedication to promoting a "Great Society." The Elementary and Secondary Education Act and the revision of the Vocational Rehabilitation Act both took effect in 1965 and addressed a wide range of educational and vocational issues related to disability. Over the next ten years, the Johnson and Nixon administrations continued expanding the federal role in establishing and funding public policy toward disability through laws as well as executive edicts. Such efforts culminated in the passage of PL 94-142, The Education for All Handicapped Children Act of 1975, signed in November of that year by President Gerald Ford. This landmark piece of legislation marked a turning point in efforts to support all children with disabilities and integrate them more fully and effectively in schools and in society. Similar state laws passed during the late 1960s and early 1970s also expanded government involvement in the lives of the disabled, with special education provisions especially relevant to the lives of children.[3]

In addition to legislative and executive actions, the federal courts played a significant role in shaping public policy and practice toward disabled youth. The *Brown v. Board of Education of Topeka* decision in 1954 heralded the onset of the civil rights movement that the Eisenhower, Kennedy, and Johnson administrations supported through various means. Disability joined race, gender, and even childhood as categories of the human condition that needed—and demanded—equal protection under the law. The stipulation in the *Brown* decision that segregated facilities are "inherently unequal" not only led to racially integrated schools but also to a series of court decisions expanding the rights of the disabled in school and society. High-profile decisions from the early 1970s such as *PARC v. Pennsylvania, Lau v. Nichols, Wyatt v. Stickney, Larry P. v. Riles, Diana v. State Board of Education,* and *Mills v. Board of Education of the District of Columbia* definitively established the civil rights of disabled children in schools and other public facilities and mandated equitable treatment in as normalized settings as possible. For the most part, state courts established similar guidelines and mandates.[4]

ADVOCACY GROUPS AND THE DISABILITY RIGHTS MOVEMENT

Advocacy groups also played a significant role in enhancing the rights and opportunities for children with disabilities in the United States during the 1960s and 1970s. The National Association for Retarded Children, which changed its name to the National Association for Retarded Citizens in 1973, and the Council for Exceptional Children (CEC) assumed leading roles in efforts to lobby, mediate, and otherwise advocate for disabled children in a variety of public and private arenas. NARC worked closely with the Kennedy and later the Johnson administrations to provide expertise, counsel, and funding on behalf of children with mental retardation. NARC members consistently served on presidential panels dedicated to addressing mental retardation in society. The organization also engaged in a massive effort to offer advice and counsel to all parties affected by or involved with mental disability, especially professionals and parents. For example, in 1971 NARC published a compilation of "Policy Statements on the Education of Mentally Retarded Children." The statements addressed a variety of issues related to education, services, residential institutions, and terminology. On the other hand, the CEC involved itself more directly in issues related to special education as its membership consisted largely of teachers and other special education professionals. Although occasionally criticized for not showing enough concern for children and too much for its own status and prestige, the CEC did address a range of important issues related to special education and the school lives of all children with disabilities.[5]

While certainly vocal and assertive, the NARC and the CEC represented mainstream thought and practice in supporting the rights of the disabled in the United States. Other groups and individuals, however, took a more activist and confrontational approach to such efforts. This amalgam of advocates advanced their agendas under the collective banner of the Disability Rights Movement. This movement represented a natural outcome of the widespread efforts to strengthen the rights of the disabled through established but often slow-acting or unresponsive entities such as governments, courts, and school districts.

The Disability Rights Movement was not only concerned with children but with all age groups and all categories of disability. It addressed workplaces and schools, public and private agencies, specific and general disabling conditions. The advocacy methods of the movement drew considerably from those used by supporters of feminism, racial and ethnic empowerment, and antiwar activism. It caught the public's attention but also alienated many in the process. The Disability Rights Movement, begun in the early 1970s, met—and continues to meet—with mixed success. Nevertheless, its role in raising the voices of persons with disabilities has enriched social and cultural understandings of disability and directed attention to many—including children—whose voices have been stifled, condemned, or ignored.[6]

SPECIAL EDUCATION: DEVELOPMENTS IN THE FIELD

Amid such truly dramatic developments in federal involvement, court action, and organized advocacy on behalf of disabled children, the world of special education—a central feature of a disabled child's experience—continued to expand and evolve. Special education professionals expressed confidence that improving special education meant identifying more children to benefit from it, training more teachers to provide it, and procuring more money to spend on it. Consequently, they continued to press local school districts and state departments of education to enhance support for all aspects of special education for children with disabilities. While exact numbers are difficult to come by given significant variations among states and districts in terms of collecting data, it is certainly safe to say that the numbers of students, teachers, classes, schools, and dollars devoted to special education in both public and private settings increased markedly during the 1960s and 1970s. School districts used increasingly sophisticated technology and test instruments to identify eligible students more accurately and effectively. The link between poverty, minority status, and special education eligibility attracted considerable attention even before 1960. As a result, the conflation of the murky distinctions between and among "at risk," "disadvantaged," "culturally deprived," and "handicapped" youngsters contributed to the increase in both numbers and investments in special education. Furthermore, more effective differentiation among existing categories of disability as well as the "creation" of new categories—such as the "birth" of learning disabilities and its baptism by Samuel Kirk at a 1963 conference, as will be discussed later in the chapter—solidified the necessity of an expansive special education empire. Special education thus continued to expand its now vital role in public schools. Disability itself became increasingly visible to professionals, politicians, and civic leaders throughout the 1960s and 1970s. Both critiques and defenses of fundamental policies and practices in special education involving identification, placement (especially concerning segregation from or integration with the "normal" peers of disabled children in public schools), and curriculum defined this era as one of remarkable energy and debate.[7]

One of the central and most controversial aspects of discourse on children with disabilities centered on the purposes, functions, and characteristics of that long-time agency for the disabled: the residential institution. Once again, institutions for the mentally disabled constituted the primary targets of such discussions. Despite the exposés of the 1940s, these facilities continued to grow in both number and size. Regrettably, little was done to alleviate the overcrowding and poor staffing of the existing institutions or prevent similar conditions from developing in new ones. Many of these institutions were renamed "training schools" or "developmental centers" in an attempt to improve their public image and indicate a return to a more educative purpose and function. Nevertheless, most continued to provide little more than custodial care. Children in such institutions now consisted mostly of those with serious levels of mental retardation. As the testimonial literature mentioned in the previous chapter reveals, institutionalization of family members, especially children, was acknowledged and admitted by members of all socioeconomic classes. As parents, regardless of their wealth, accepted clearly degrading facilities as appropriate settings for all seriously mentally disabled children, there was a rapid growth of new construction. Seventy-five percent of public residential institutions existing in 1970 had been built after 1950.[8]

According to some historians, however, this rapid expansion set the stage for the eventual dismantling of most such institutions beginning in the 1970s. The conditions at some of the most famous asylums for the mentally retarded deteriorated as states admitted many more children and adults than they could serve adequately. Underfunding and poorly trained staff persisted. "In this context," wrote historian James Trent, "brutality, exploitation, neglect, and routinized boredom were too often the rule, not the exception."[9] The most devastating documentation of these conditions came in the form of a photographic essay: Burton Blatt and Fred Kaplan's shocking *Christmas in Purgatory: A Photographic Essay on Mental Retardation*. Published in 1966, *Christmas in Purgatory* depicted hundreds of children (including infants and toddlers) as well as adults in institutions in wretched, dehumanizing environments. Even photographs of children in school and play situations that appeared clean and safe were coupled with captions that suggested these children deserved much better. The names of the photographed institutions were not revealed, underscoring the fact that these conditions could have existed—and likely did—almost anywhere. "Although our pictures could not even begin to capture the total and overwhelming horror we saw, smelled, and felt, they represent a side of America that has rarely been shown to the general public and is little understood by most of us," wrote Blatt in his introduction to the book. "Our 'Christmas in Purgatory' brought us to the depths of despair. We now have a deep sorrow, one that will not abate until the American people are aware of—and do something about—the treatment of the severely mentally retarded in our state institutions."[10]

Christmas in Purgatory was not alone in its attempt to bring awareness of and justice to residential institutions for the mentally disabled. Senator Robert F. Kennedy addressed the New York State legislature in 1965, deploring the conditions of the Rome and Willowbrook facilities in his state. A Danish visitor to the Sonoma State Hospital in California decried the terrible conditions there, claiming in a widely read article that "in our country, we would not be allowed to treat cattle like that."[11] In 1972, investigative journalist Geraldo Rivera turned television cameras to the Letchworth and Willowbrook facilities, exposing the degradation within and comparing them to Nazi death camps. Spurred on by a movement within disability rights and special education groups during the late 1960s and early 1970s that stressed "normalization" and "deinstitutionalization," public exposés shouted the same emphatic message: These facilities must close.[12]

Given the extreme financial burden these institutions created on public coffers as well as the intensely negative publicity surrounding the institutions themselves, closing them proved an attractive option. Supported by the theory and philosophy of the normalization movement led by noted psychologist Wolf Wolfensberger and by former NARC leaders Gunnar and Rosemary Dybwad, initiatives to close the institutions and relocate the residents to community-based shelters, halfway houses, and other local service centers proceeded apace. Through the 1970s and into the 1980s, states closed a multitude of such facilities or at least drastically reduced their residential populations. States considered such efforts an economic windfall: they were no longer required to pour so much money into these facilities, while federal government programs funded much of the process of movement to community-based facilities. Residents who relocated to community-based services demonstrated that they could function in society. While the repercussions of the normalization movement have been far too complex to address adequately here, deinstitutionalization has led to profound changes in both the nature and quality of services provided to the mentally disabled—for better and for worse.[13]

Significantly, deinstitutionalization did not strike similar blows to the existence and support of residential institutions for the deaf and for the blind. These facilities had never been subjected to the intense scrutiny given to those for the mentally disabled. Much of the difference had to do with both the status and nature of their respective disabilities as well as the size, condition, and purposes of the institutions that served the various groups. The modality deficits of deafness and blindness were much less prevalent in the population than the socially constructed concept of mental retardation, so issues of overcrowding did not plague the schools for the deaf and blind to the extent that they did the institutions for the mentally disabled. Although children who were deaf and blind were typically seen as helpless or pitiable, their normal level of intelligence was never questioned. Neither was their family background consistently linked to alleged "inferior" groups of people, as typically happened for those considered mentally retarded. Institutions for the deaf and the blind never abandoned their *educational* essence: the idea that they were schools, not caretaking facilities. Specially trained teachers and staff served these children and supported their instruction much more effectively than did staff in the facilities for the mentally disabled. The residents of institutions for the deaf and for the blind thus were viewed as more capable, more attractive, and more worthy of state support. This is not to say that such facilities were free from controversy, inadequacies, or abuse; they were not. However, the "in-house" institutional histories noted in an earlier chapter, and the annual reports prepared by the superintendents of the institutions, painted a picture of accomplishment, dedication, and professionalism that satisfied most interested parties. Although long challenged for the segregation they create and defend, most of these institutions continue to thrive to this day.[14]

VOICES FOR AND OF THE DISABLED: ADVICE FOR PARENTS

Such enormous and fundamental changes in the world of special education and disability had dramatic effects on the day-to-day lives of children and families living with disability. Until the 1950s very little was known or revealed about the daily lives of disabled children and their parents; public and professional discussions of their condition and prospects surrounded but rarely included them. With the advent of "confessional" literature and the rise of local organizations advocating for persons with disabilities, however, the public began to hear more from those directly affected by disability.[15]

As a premier advocacy organization, the NARC sought to enlighten, inform, and counsel not only the public but also those directly affected by disability. After its formal organization in 1950, NARC began publishing extensively. Many of its publications advised parents on how best to cope with their child's mental disability. From the 1950s to the 1960s, NARC prepared or distributed a plethora of material by and for parents to help them do the best they could for their mentally retarded child. A review of this material offers a glimpse into the world of the child and the family that is more personal than that typically provided in the professional literature.

First and foremost, the NARC publications addressed the process parents typically went through when informed their child was mentally retarded. Shock, dismay, and heartache often surfaced upon learning about the child's condition. Feelings of guilt, shame, anger, and especially denial often followed these reactions. Several publications reassured parents that such feelings were normal and understandable. Betty Hansen, a Michigan parent who wrote frequently about raising mentally retarded children, reminded her fellow parents that "retardation at its best is a social problem of staggering magnitude.... It is one of the great tragedies of nature and a personal catastrophe to those directly involved." Hansen prefaced these comments by proclaiming that "I can only thank God that this tragedy happened to me just once" and that her feelings were perfectly normal.[16] Whether the child was diagnosed at birth or not until her or his developmental delays become obvious, the effect upon learning for the first time that "your child is retarded" often proved devastating. Wrote one mother, "I was sitting, vegetable-like, in a chair, staring at the pattern of the rug, mired in self-pity. Helplessly, hopelessly, trying to escape our problem."[17] Nancy Storie, a mother who at first "refused to accept this repugnant idea," admitted that "the shock seemed too much to endure.... I was filled with remorse and crying spells. The thoughts that entered my mind—even suicide or disposing of the child—were but a small part of the adjustment which faced me." Almost every parent hearing the news felt "stunned," "alone," or "resign[ed]...to a cruel blow dealt by chance."[18]

Accordingly, all parties had to be prepared to address the situation with sympathy and realism. According to several professionals, one of the first steps parents needed to take was to accept the reality of their situation and resolve to adjust to it for the benefit of the family and especially the child. A pamphlet published by the staff of the Vineland Training School in New Jersey stated that parents' "own attitude toward their retarded child is the essential element that determines his future. No future can exist for a child until his parents accept the fact that he is retarded.... *True acceptance means that they will love their child and do everything possible to help him. Thereby they become an important force in leading him to a place in society*" (emphasis in the original). However, the pamphlet also cautioned: "It is not easy. For the parents of a mentally retarded child must express a tolerance and love far greater than is demanded of the parents of normal children.... Otherwise, a child realizes that something about him is not right in the eyes of those closest to him—and thereby his problems increase."[19] Dr. Leo Kanner, a leader in the field of mental retardation in the 1960s, compared this "mature acknowledgement of the actuality and acceptance of the child" with that of parents who "search for either scapegoats ... [or] magic cures" or who completely denied "the existence of any retardation." The latter reactions, according to Kanner, required a "'thorough overhauling' in the direction of mature acceptance."[20] Nancy Storie went through each of these stages. "After I could think rationally, I detested my thoughts and myself for thinking them.... As long as Lisa was placed on this earth, perhaps she was meant to help people better understand a child of her circumstances. She was not to be discarded like an old shoe.... It is every person's right to be treated with respect and loved."[21] This process of acceptance often helped to resolve an essential question that so many parents had to answer: "Why did this happen to us?"[22]

Once parents had accepted their child as one who needs and deserves complete love, they needed to learn more about not only the condition of mental retardation but also the many ways to care for the child and enhance her or his learning opportunities. Indeed, one assumption about why parents experienced such shock and denial on learning of their child's disability was "the obvious fact that many parents come face to face with the diagnosis of mental retardation without ever having heard the term used or having seen such a child to their knowledge."[23] By learning about the condition itself as well as the many approaches to teaching and caring for mentally retarded youth, parents could offer positive support and effective assistance. Of course, providing such information constituted a core mission of the NARC. In 1959, NARC produced an extensive reading list for parents that covered such topics as "You Are Not Alone," "What Do We Do Now," "Using Resources Outside the Home," and "The Broad Picture." Some materials spoke directly to parents about the best ways to teach children skills such as eating, dressing, personal hygiene, speaking, and walking. Others advised parents on ways to discipline, entertain, and socialize their retarded child. In addition, parents heard and read extensive advice on coping with more intangible issues such as "How Can I Face My Family and Friends" and "What It Means to Have a Retarded Child." NARC also reprinted materials addressing other universal issues such as the child's relations with siblings; the child's sexual and religious development; how to prepare for the day the child leaves home; and how to ensure the child's well-being after her or his parents have died. NARC's goal was to reduce parental frustration and uncertainty while promoting positive aspects of persons with mental retardation, especially children. This was important because, NARC alleged, such children "cannot speak for themselves, cannot ask for the special training and help they require. . . . [NARC] works for them."[24]

Effectively educating parents also required that they understand and appreciate the role of the physician in providing care for their disabled child. The family doctor or pediatrician usually was the individual who informed the parents about their child's disability. Furthermore, much of the advice dispensed in the literature on raising a retarded child included a constant reminder that "your doctor will tell you" about proper procedure and that the advice of responsible medical professionals could and should be trusted. NARC clearly recommended that all parents place their child under the care of a medical professional, seek referrals for evaluation through that professional, and then "follow the treatment plan and recommendations for continuing medical supervision and programs for education, training and development."[25] In the late 1960s Mrs. Max Murray, President of the Virginia Association for Retarded Children, observed: "The professional person, by the very nature of his training is primarily concerned with finding a solution to the problem immediately at hand—and this is as it should be." Murray included doctors and psychologists as well as teachers and social workers in the category of professional.[26] In an article entitled "Helping the Parents of a Retarded Child" two Kansas doctors noted that "the physician who will take the time to listen, to understand, to support, and to counsel parents of the retarded child will do them a great service."[27]

Despite such confidence in the role of medical professionals, the relationship between doctor and family could become strained—if not combative—unless parents and physicians paid close attention to the sensibilities and responsibilities of the other party. One of the most constant complaints from parents about the process of identification and treatment was that their family doctor or pediatrician failed to appreciate the parents' personal anguish, avoided or delayed delivering a confident and timely diagnosis of mental retardation, and ignored parents' need for honesty and compassion. Parents also expressed dismay at the lack of knowledge many medical professionals exhibited when trying to figure out what was "wrong" with the child. Some parents complained of doctors who did not want to be "bothered" or who "were impatient and annoyed" at the parents' concern and assertiveness. Others allegedly made parents feel guilty or ashamed or contemptible; some physicians were accused of "brushing" them off and "pushing" them around the health care system. As two doctors from the Menninger Clinic in Kansas casually understated, "parents who are angry because 'the doctor looked at our child and said he was retarded and needed to be put away' have been approached in a way that is not helpful to them." NARC and other advocates for mentally retarded children also cautioned parents to avoid unethical and unqualified "doctors"—"quacks," as NARC described them—who often took advantage of parents' false hopes and promised expensive quick cures or guaranteed "special" treatments that would make the retardation simply go away. In the 1960s, even if parents avoided unqualified "quacks," they faced not only their own uncertainties and inadequacies but also those of other professionals who tried to perform their duties but lacked the knowledge, skills, or dispositions to do so effectively.[28]

In addition to the often traumatic nature of relationships with professionals, parents faced a difficult and complex decision once a child reached school age, if not sooner: whether to keep the child at home or send her or him to an institution. The decision involved not only the child's education but also judgments about her or his social, emotional, and physical environment. It also placed parents in the position of choosing whether to continue the taxing responsibility of caring for the child or risking the psychological toll of "putting him away" for years, perhaps for ever. "The emotions are deeply involved, and the decision is all the more difficult because no answer fits every case," wrote Katharine G. Ecob, Executive Secretary of the New York State Committee on Mental Hygiene. "Parents who send their child to an institution love him as much as do parents who keep theirs at home. It is not a question of love or duty, but of expediency. What is best for all concerned?" Ecob believed that the decision must rest on considerations of the welfare of "the retarded child . . . of the family . . . [and] of society."[29] Miriam Lernerd of the Bureau of Mental Deficiency in New Jersey added that "mental retardation, in itself, is not sufficient reason to put a child in an institution." The child's home environment, physical and mental capabilities, eventual vocational needs (if any), and parental resources—especially financial—also factored into such decisions. The ultimate goal, simply put, was for parents to do "the best they can for their child."[30]

NARC proved quite sensitive to the ambivalence most parents experienced in reaching this decision. The organization distributed reprints and publications from the 1950s through the mid-1960s addressing these concerns, offering counsel and identifying issues to consider. These articles reviewed concerns such as the "normal" social life of the family, the presence of viable day school or public school alternatives, the accessibility and prestige of a given institution, the demands on parents' financial and physical resources, and the nature and extent of a child's disability. In these documents, institutions are painted as viable and decent alternatives to home life. Parents were advised to inspect a facility before commitment, but none of the serious concerns and conditions verified by exposés or other commentaries were mentioned. NARC also prepared through its Public Institutions Committee a set of guidelines for "creating better relationship between parents and institutions." These guidelines described procedures to be expected, questions to ask, and suggestions to be followed by parents in the event they chose to institutionalize their child.[31] Betty Hansen, the parent who wrote frequently for her local NARC newsletter, attempted to comfort parents who chose institutionalization. "This day of parting with their handicapped child was not arrived at lightly," she wrote in describing one family. "For a long time his parents would not even consider it at all. Then they considered it a little. Finally they were able to consider it fully . . . wondering if they could ever find the courage." The parents in Hansen's story determined it was best for "*this* child, if not for others." She offered that "each of our children must reach a season of maturity, of growing up and going away. And if we love them we would not have it otherwise. There is a day of departure for every child under the sun." By the late 1960s, however, NARC ceased distributing such supportive calls for institutionalization, as it became aware of the horrendous conditions found in so many facilities and attuned to the rising call for more community-based residential settings for children with serious mental disability.[32]

THE STATUS OF CHILDREN IN SPECIAL EDUCATION: THE 1970s

Special education found itself in a state of upheaval on several fronts beginning in the late 1960s. Discussions about mental retardation and the most effective ways to address it in schools, institutions, and the community dominated much of the discourse regarding disability. Lloyd Dunn, a prominent American scholar in the study and practice of mental retardation, published an article in 1968 challenging the notion that segregated special education was necessary for all children identified as mentally retarded. The article created a furor among special educators and other school professionals. Within five years, a sizable group of special educators were challenging a variety of aspects of special education, ranging from processes of identification to curriculum development, teacher training, school and classroom organization, and the self-perpetuating and self-justifying tendencies of special education itself. The growing presence of children with all kinds of disabling conditions in the public schools strained public education and emboldened special educators. From 1968 on, the professional literature featured energetic and often heated debates on a wide range of issues related to the education of children with disabilities.[33]

Contributing further to the dynamism and complexity of special education was the development of a new and often mystifying category of disability. Samuel Kirk's naming of "learning disabilities" in 1963 helped special educators target and address the special education needs of children whose struggles in school previously had not fallen under existing categories of disability and thus had not been formally recognized and categorized. The subsequent establishment of learning disabilities as a recognized, unique category for disabled children further expanded the reach of special education, generating more dollars and more attention from all corners of the world of public schooling. By the early 1980s, learning disabilities had become the single largest category of disability recognized under federal law.[34]

For children identified as having learning disabilities—and their parents—the world of special education constituted a relatively new and perplexing environment. Many such children had never experienced life as a special education student, and special educators and researchers struggled to understand the origins and manifestations of this complex and still mysterious disability. In an effort similar to NARC's work in supporting and advising parents of children with mental retardation, specialists and others experienced in the realm of learning disabilities also prepared guides designed to ensure appropriate education for disabled children. One of these, *Something's Wrong with My Child: A Parents' Book about Children with Learning Disabilities*, appeared in 1973 and shed some light on how learning disabled children, their families, and schools interacted to address this condition.[35]

As a relatively new category of disability, learning disabilities presented some stark challenges to regular classroom teachers as well as special educators. Much of the advice directed toward parents therefore emphasized the uncertainty and inconsistencies that likely faced learning disabled children as they began to navigate the structures and practices of special education. Parents were reminded that learning disabilities constituted a mostly school-based or school-induced disability that only became readily apparent once an average or even "bright" child began to struggle in school. Such struggles, according to experts, could well result in behaviors that rejected or defied assistance from adults or challenged appropriate standards of behavior. Teachers were cautioned to be careful what to say to poorly performing children who seemed to be merely lazy or uncooperative but were in fact disabled. Parents and teachers were advised to work cooperatively and patiently with each other for the children's sake and to respect the merits and drawbacks of both segregated and integrated programs, based on a given child's individual needs and strengths. The limited number of effective public school programs led to the establishment of a multitude of private schools for children with learning disabilities, and parents were directed to these if they experienced a lack of success in or cooperation from the public schools. The overall view showed children, parents, and teachers feeling their way both into and through the world of special education and the consequences of being labeled "handicapped."[36]

Caught amid this ferment in special education were the children with special needs, living and participating day to day in hospitals, homes, residential institutions, segregated day schools, separate classes, and even regular classrooms. Supposedly the ultimate beneficiaries of these far-reaching and complicated dynamics affecting special education, these children often became lost amid the debates, experiments, statistics, laws, and court decisions. For example, a multitude of studies had been conducted since the early 1960s on the effects of various instructional settings, curricular adjustments, and classroom management systems on children within the schools. These studies attempted to ascertain the social acceptance, academic success, and personal growth of disabled children in special education programs. However, these research projects revealed barely anything about the students themselves, focusing instead on aggregated data, statistical analyses, and hypothesis acceptance or rejection. To review them is to examine the lived experiences of literally thousands of students and yet to learn little if anything about them as children.[37]

Fortunately, by the early 1970s those involved in the lives of such children were producing narratives and other material that revealed some of what was going on inside these spaces—although the silence of voice from the students themselves remained telling. Interestingly, the voices of persons who were deaf and/or blind gained much more notoriety and visibility, largely through personal memoirs and testimonials published in book form. Throughout the 1900s, persons who were deaf and/or blind published narratives detailing their experiences and challenges in society. Adults almost always wrote these, but some of their recollections focused on childhood events or on their struggles as parents learning to live with a disabled child. Helen Keller's immensely popular autobiography *The Story of My Life* (1903) verified early on the public's interest in at least some of the thoughts of disabled persons. Others followed, and by late in the century the life stories and perspectives of persons who were deaf or blind had become available to a wide audience.[38]

Through the 1970s, narratives depicting the world of children who were deaf focused on issues of compatibility with the cultures of the school and the community. Much discussion centered on the comparative value of segregated or integrated instructional settings, that is, whether or not deaf children should be included in regular classrooms. Of course this issue had dominated conversations about deaf education since the introduction of oralism and public day schools for the deaf in the latter part of the nineteenth century. At its heart rested the fundamental question of the importance of continuing and strengthening the traditions and integrity of a distinct deaf culture and community. The nature of the issue itself extended from the political to the personal. Parents and students commented on frequent feelings of isolation and misunderstanding when situated in inclusive settings. One handbook offering advice to parents of deaf youngsters encouraged integration if the conditions were right. However, it also cautioned that "integrating a deaf child into a regular classroom . . . can do irreparable harm unless the child clearly demonstrates the communication and academic ability to progress on equal terms with his peers."[39] This advice compared interestingly with statements of other researchers that hard of hearing students do better academically over the long term in a mainstreamed setting because of higher expectations than do similar students in a segregated setting where expectations for achievement were apparently lower. These researchers also stated, however, that a child with profound or complete hearing loss almost always "needs his special teachers and programs if the entire experience is not to be an unmitigated disaster for him." Such comments revealed the complexity and ambivalence—indeed the "inconclusive and contradictory" state—of making appropriate decisions about integrating children with hearing impairments in regular classrooms.[40]

Deaf persons themselves and their families expressed the same kind of ambivalence and variety of perspectives regarding these issues. From the difficult process of learning that one's child is deaf to making decisions about that child's future, parents often struggled with finding the "right" answers to their questions and concerns. For example, in the book *Deaf Like Me*, Thomas and Louise Spradley recounted an uncomfortable yet highly informative meeting with parents of other deaf children attending the Starr King Exceptional School for children with speech and hearing impairments in Sacramento, California. Discussions of problems with discipline, communication, and academics made it clear that their child, Lynn, not only experienced problems with being deaf but also with just being a child. The Spradleys' involvement with the school's decision to replace a pure oralist approach with one that also included finger-spelling and the use of sign language was particularly revealing of the heated controversy within the deaf community itself, especially among hearing parents of deaf children. Considering all the issues raised at these meetings, they poignantly observed, "Several roads fanned out in front of us. All seemed to hold great risks for Lynn. We fell asleep long after midnight, anxious and troubled about the future." As Lynn reported:

> I wanted to go to Berkeley. My parents didn't want me to go away to school. They wanted me to stay at home and attend a mainstream class at a nearby school. But I wanted more friends and teachers I could communicate with easily. English and math were hard for me to understand, and when I came home I didn't have any friends my age who were deaf. My brother, Bruce, had lots of friends. Sometimes I got frustrated and angry or lost my temper.

When the Starr King School hired Linda Raymond, a deaf teacher who used sign language, she helped convince Lynn's parents to send her to the California School for the Deaf in Berkeley.[41]

In the book's epilogue, Lynn described how their decision to send her to the residential state school—where, as she said, "everyone could sign!"— served as a turning point in her life. "Some of my classmates [at the residential school] remembered going to schools like mine where they were not allowed to sign. We thought that was stupid. We felt lucky we had learned to sign and could discuss things so easily.... Deaf people are not dumb. Deaf kids are just as smart as hearing kids. With sign language deaf kids can do anything." Lynn's support of a very traditional yet still controversial approach to deaf education and communication demonstrated that this controversy about learning and lifestyle was still very much alive and significant during the late twentieth century—just as it had been one hundred years earlier.[42]

Children who were blind faced similar differences of opinion regarding the optimum setting for their education and socialization. Once again, the question of whether a residential institution or a day school offered the best opportunities for blind children to learn and to grow dominated much of the discourse during this period. By the mid-1960s many residential institutions for the blind offered opportunities for students to extend their education beyond the walls of the institution. Some joined Boy or Girl Scouts, others attended Sunday Schools and many used community recreational facilities such as parks and swimming pools. Many more children had the opportunity to return home for weekends, holidays, and vacation periods because of advances in modes of transportation. On the other hand, public school services such as day schools or special classes for blind or partially sighted children existed in districts where size and resources could support them, as they had for generations. The use of itinerant teachers—specialists in teaching blind children who were assigned to an entire district, not just one school—expanded public school opportunities for children with vision impairments, especially in terms of one-on-one instruction. They also allowed such children to spend more time in a regular classroom.[43]

Debate continued as to the various academic and social advantages and disadvantages of residential versus public school settings. As earlier, the opportunity to live at home with one's family remained a strong advantage of public day school instruction. The inclusion of blind youngsters in regular nursery schools and kindergartens garnered praise from experts as a sound way to familiarize "normal" children with their blind peers and to accept them more readily. In theory, this effect carried into the regular grades. Even so, some experts commented that attending public school in segregated classes "defeats the very purpose for which [the segregated class] was established.... The segregated class cannot possibly offer to its children the equipment, the variety of experiences, and the supplementary instruction which they would get in a residential school." Special schools for the blind had technology specific to the condition of blindness; specially trained teachers; resources for work in art, music, and language arts; and physical as well as vocational education programs designed specifically for blind children.[44]

Of utmost concern to parents and families was taking advantage of opportunities to socialize their blind children effectively. Such efforts of course started soon after birth and/or after identifying the child as blind or visually impaired.

One 1975 publication entitled *Get a Wiggle On* was written in the voice of the infant/child. It began, "It's a fact. I have a visual problem. I may be seriously handicapped by it.... But with your help, I will think about my problems a great deal less than others do. After all, not seeing so well—or not seeing at all—is normal for me." The child then suggests various ways for parents and caretakers to ensure constant physical, emotional, and cognitive engagement for the child. "Please tie together all these separate pieces of incoming information for me. Tell me what I am touching, smelling, tasting, hearing, and seeing. I need to be talked to—to learn language [and] so that I will know that I am a part of things.... I've got to wiggle so that later I'll be able to Move it!"[45] Another guide for parents, this published in 1977, noted that "the blind child cannot see where the other children are or what they are doing. He does not know if they would welcome or reject his presence because he is not receiving any visual messages from them; nor, for that matter, does he send any." The guide suggested that parents (and teachers) compensate for the blind child's natural passivity by offering suggestions and directions to both the blind child and her seeing peers to help them interact effectively. Finally, the matter of overwork could become important and ultimately counterproductive. "Sometimes there is very little opportunity for fun in the life of a blind child. People are so anxious for him to learn skills and to do things right that life tends to be too earnest," the authors advised. "He needs to learn from the other children how to be silly and corny and giggle about things grown-ups don't understand." The cognitive, affective, and physical challenges faced by a child who was blind not only complicated the learning and growth of the child but also required great care and sensitivity on the part of friends and adults who were important parts of her or his life.[46]

THE LIVES OF CHILDREN WITH DISABILITIES: ANTICIPATING THE FUTURE

With federal legislation mandating once and for all the need for public schools to do much more to accommodate children with disabilities, the status of persons with disabilities in schools and society garnered increasing attention from professionals as well as the public. Central to such discussions was the issue of integrating ("mainstreaming," in the then-current terminology) students with disabilities into regular schools and classrooms. This topic had received significant attention for decades as a "should we or shouldn't we" question. With PL 94-142, it became a "how much and in what ways" question: the law required it but was not specific or clear on exactly how far school districts were expected to proceed in terms of accommodating all students with all kinds of disabilities and levels of intervention needs.

Furthermore, questions and concerns involved much more than just practical matters of implementation. In his 1979 book *The Quiet Revolution: The Struggle for the Rights of Disabled Americans,* James Haskins noted the benefits of attending regular public school for children such as Michelle Duffy, a 13-year-old born with spina bifida (a congenital disorder that literally means "open spine"), or Eileen, a young child who was blind but whose interactions with "normal" children brought the world much closer to her. For many, the issue of mainstreaming had become one of ethical imperative more than effective schooling: full integration with the rest of the world was now possible after generations of marginalization and segregation, and it was time to press the issue. Moreover, limiting such opportunities to school-age children was no longer defensible. Haskins called for education to be redefined as "an open-ended continuum available from the cradle to the grave that serves individual needs." As expressed in "A Bill of Rights for the Handicapped" prepared by the United Cerebral Palsy Association, "the handicapped individual has the right to education to the fullest extent to which he is intellectually capable, provided through the regular channels of American education."[47]

Other matters related to the lives of children with disabilities also loomed large. Calls for advocating for disabled children increased. So did demands that schools and social services rethink their policies and practices to recognize more fully the rights of the disabled to a full, active, and authentically participatory life in society. In an article published in the *Peabody Journal of Education* in 1973, Douglas Biklen, who would become a major figure in redefining the role of special education in the public schools in the last two decades of the twentieth century, told the story of one family's struggles to gain attention, let alone dignity and respect, from politicians, the legal system, and the school district. Biklen argued that their story "testifies to the difficulties disabled children encounter when they seek their right to service. . . . If this case serves no other purpose, it should encourage us to question and, indeed, challenge special educational services and policies which promote categorization, segregation and, ultimately, institutionalization." From 1980 on, this challenge was accepted and addressed by a wide range of persons with disabilities and their advocates, with the lives and welfare of disabled children at the core of the conversation. The final chapter of this book examines efforts at the end of the twentieth century to assist children with disabilities.[48]

NOTES

1. President's Committee on Mental Retardation, *MR 76: Mental Retardation; Past and Present* (Washington, DC, 1977), 52–54, 83–96.

2. Ibid., 84–96; Margret Winzer, *The History of Special Education: From Isolation to Integration* (Washington, DC, 1993), 376–78; R. C. Scheerenberger, *A History of Mental Retardation* (Baltimore, MD, 1983), 247–49.

3. President's Committee on Mental Retardation, *MR 76: Mental Retardation*, 85–98; Winzer, *History of Special Education*, 380–82; Scheerenberger, *History of Mental Retardation*, 251–52. For a detailed discussion of federal and state law pertaining to disability and special education for children, see Nikki Murdick, Barbara Gartin, and Terry Crabtree, *Special Education Law* (Upper Saddle River, NJ, 2002), and Erwin L. Levine and Elizabeth M. Wexler, *PL 94-142: An Act of Congress* (New York, 1981).

4. Murdick, Gartin, and Crabtree, *Special Education Law*, 10–13; President's Committee on Mental Retardation, *MR 76: Mental Retardation*, 100–1; Robert L. Osgood, *The History of Inclusion in the United States* (Washington, DC, 2005), 103–6; Levine and Wexler, *PL 94-142*, 38–41.

5. President's Committee on Mental Retardation, *MR 76: Mental Retardation*, 38–61, 69–76; M. Stephen Lilly, "A Teapot in a Tempest," *Exceptional Children* 37 (September 1970): 45–47; Winzer, *History of Special Education*, 335–36.

6. Osgood, *History of Inclusion in the United States*, 129–33. For detailed discussions of the Disability Rights Movement, see Sharon Barnartt and Richard Scotch, *Disability Protests: Contentious Politics 1970–1999* (Washington, DC, 2001); Jacqueline Vaughn Switzer, *Disabled Rights: American Disability Policy and the Fight for Equality* (Washington, DC, 2003); Duane F. Stroman, *The Disability Rights Movement: From Deinstitutionalization to Self-Determination* (Lanham, MD, 2003); and Doris Zames Fleischer and Freida Zames, *The Disability Rights Movement: From Charity to Confrontation* (Philadelphia, PA, 2001).

7. Osgood, *History of Inclusion in the United States*, 62–109; Winzer, *History of Special Education*, 356–60, 376–85. See also Barry M. Franklin, *From "Backwardness" to "At-Risk": Childhood Learning Difficulties and the Contradictions of School Reform* (Albany, NY, 1994), for lengthy and illuminating discussions of many of these issues and topics. For a brief but informative federal statement on the relation of environment to mental retardation see the President's Committee on Mental Retardation, "Hello World," GPO 1968-0-308-222 (Washington, DC, 1986), an information pamphlet describing the status of mental retardation in the country and the public's need to address it.

8. James W. Trent Jr., *Inventing the Feeble Mind: A History of Mental Retardation in the United States* (Berkeley, CA, 1994), 237–38, 266; Scheerenberger, *History of Mental Retardation*, 252.

9. Trent, *Inventing the Feeble Mind*, 238, 255.

10. Burton Blatt and Fred Kaplan, *Christmas in Purgatory: A Photographic Essay on Mental Retardation* (Boston, MA, 1966), vi.

11. Quoted in Trent, *Inventing the Feeble Mind*, 255—61.

12. Scheerenberger, *History of Mental Retardation*, 252–53; Osgood, *History of Inclusion in the United States*, 93–96. See also David J. Rothman and Sheila M. Rothman, *The Willowbrook Wars: A Decade of Struggle for Social Justice* (New York, 1984), for a thorough case study of how the deinstitutionalization movement affected this notorious facility.

13. Trent, *Inventing the Feeble Mind*, 261–68; Scheerenberger, *History of Mental Retardation*, 253; Rothman and Rothman, passim. The seminal document explaining normalization is Wolf Wolfensberger, *The Principle of Normalization in Human Services* (Toronto, ON, 1972). See William Sloan and Harvey A. Stevens, *A Century of Decision: A History of the American Association on Mental Deficiency 1876–1976* (Washington, DC, 1976), 296–97, for a look at deinstitutionalization from a historical perspective.

14. Most of the state-supported residential schools for deaf and for blind children publish annual reports that are available in public archives. See also Walter B. Hendrickson, *From Shelter to Self-Reliance: A History of the Illinois Braille and Sight Saving School* (Jacksonville, IL, 1972) for a typical example of a generally quite positive in-house history.

15. See Trent, *Inventing the Feeble Mind*, 230–50, for a full discussion of these developments.

16. Betty Hansen, "The Face of Truth," reprinted from the Saginaw County, Michigan, *ARC Newsletter*, February 1960. Available in the ARC Files, Drawer B, of the Coleman Institute on Disability Archives, University of Colorado-Boulder.

17. Quoted in Salvatore G. DiMichael, "The Mentally Retarded Child in Home and Community," n.d., ARC Files, Drawer C.

18. "They Discovered a New Dimension of Love," reprinted from *Today's Health*, February 1959, 22 in ARC Files, Drawer D.

19. Staff of the Training School at Vineland, New Jersey, *Home Care of the Mentally Retarded Child* (Vineland, NJ, 1961), 1.

20. Leo Kanner, quoted in Mrs. Max A. Murray, "Needs of Parents of Mentally Retarded Children," 1969, ARC Files, Drawer D.

21. "They Discovered a New Dimension of Love," 24.

22. DiMichael, "The Mentally Retarded Child," 3–5.

23. Murray, "Needs of Parents," 3.

24. National Association for Retarded Children, *Windows of Understanding: A Reading List for Parents Who Are Newly Facing the Discovery of Mental Retardation in Their Child* (New York, 1959), 4–11; Willie H. Scarborough, "A Letter to Parents," 1954, ARC Files, Drawer C; Staff of the Training School, 6–25; Siegried A. Centerwall and Willard R. Centerwall, *Mental Retardation* (Loma Linda, CA, 1961), 4–5; Betty Hansen, "Day of Departure," Saginaw County *ARC Newsletter*, n.d., ARC Files, Drawer B. See also Evalyn S. Gendel, "Sex Education of the Mentally Retarded Child in the Home" (paper presented at the Council for Exceptional Children Convention, April 19, 1968, ARC Files, Drawer E); Robert A. Perske, "An Attempt to Find an Adequate Theological View of Mental Retardation" (paper presented at the Conference on "The Church and the Mentally Retarded," Nebraska Psychiatric Institute, April 1965, ARC Files, Drawer A); Meyer Schreiber and Mary Feeley, "Siblings of the Retarded," reprinted from *Children*, November–December 1965, ARC Files, Drawer E; NARC Guardianship Committee, *What Will Happen to My Child? Some Suggestions for Parents Who Are Concerned with Providing Lifetime Protection for a Retarded Son or Daughter* (New York, 1961); National Association for Retarded Children, "How to Aid the Retarded," 1962, 4, ARC Files,

Drawer C. NARC also prepared a comprehensive pamphlet for parents entitled "The Mentally Retarded . . . Their New Hope," n.d., ARC Files, Drawer C.

25. National Association for Retarded Children, *The ABC's of Quackery and Sound Medical Care: A Guide for Parents of the Mentally Retarded* (New York, 1968), 1, ARC Files, Drawer D.

26. Murray, "Needs of Parents," 6–7.

27. Keith N. Bryant and J. Cotter Hirschberg, "Helping the Parents of a Retarded Child," *American Journal of Diseases of Children* 102 (July 1961): 82.

28. Charlotte H. Waskowitz, "The Parents of Retarded Children Speak for Themselves," reprinted by NARC from the *Journal of Pediatrics* (March 1959): 4–7, ARC Files, Drawer D; Bryant and Hirschberg, "Helping the Parents of a Retarded Child," 83; Murray, "Needs of Parents," 7–10; NARC, *The ABC's of Quackery*, 2–8.

29. Katharine G. Ecob, *Deciding What's Best for Your Retarded Child* (New York, 1959), 3–4, ARC Files, Drawer B.

30. Suzanne Hart Strait, "Bringing Up a Retarded Child," reprinted from *Parents' and Better Homemaking Magazine* 37 (December 1962), n.p., ARC Files, Drawer A.

31. Strait, passim; Ecob, 8–16; National Association for Retarded Children, Public Institutions Committee, "Creating Better Relationship between Parents and Institutions" (paper presented at the Public Institutions Workshop, NARC Convention, 1958).

32. Betty Hansen, "Day of Departure," Saginaw County *ARC Newsletter*, n.d., n.p., ARC Files Drawer B.

33. Lloyd Dunn, "Special Education for the Mildly Retarded—Is Much of It Justifiable?" *Exceptional Children* 35 (September 1968): 5–22.

34. Daniel P. Hallahan and James M. Kauffman, *Exceptional Children: Introduction to Special Education*, 4th ed. (Englewood Cliffs, NJ, 1988), 100–6.

35. Milton Brutten, Sylvia O. Richardson, and Charles Mangel, *Something's Wrong with My Child: A Parents' Book about Children with Learning Disabilities* (New York, 1973).

36. Ibid., 98–118.

37. Cegelka and Tyler produced a meta-analysis of this body of research, providing an exhaustive review of such studies dating back to the 1930s. See Walter L. Cegelka and James L. Tyler, "The Efficacy of Special Class Placement for the Mentally Retarded in Proper Perspective," *Training School Bulletin* 67 (1970): 33–68. Some representative titles of this professional literature include Hollace Goodman, Jay Gottlieb, and Robert H. Harrison, "Social Acceptance of EMRs Integrated into a Nongraded Elementary School," *American Journal of Mental Deficiency* 76 (1972): 412–17; Milton Budoff and Jay Gottlieb, "Special-Class EMR Children Mainstreamed: A Study of an Aptitude (Learning Potential) × Treatment Interaction," *American Journal of Mental Deficiency* 81 (1976): 1–11; and James K. Myers, "The Efficacy of the Special Day School for EMR Pupils," *Mental Retardation* 14 (August 1976): 3–11.

38. Helen Keller, *The Story of My Life* (New York, 1903). Keller was a prolific writer throughout her adult life and came to represent for many the "Voice" of persons with disabilities. See Kim E. Nielsen, *The Radical Lives of Helen Keller* (New York, 2004), for a provocative and fascinating examination of public interpretations of Keller's persona and of her often controversial viewpoints. A comparable biography is Henry Randolph Latimer, *The Conquest of Blindness: An Autobiographical Review of the Life and Work of Henry Randolph Latimer* (New York, 1937).

39. Lee Katz, Steve L. Mathis III, and Edward C. Merrill Jr., *The Deaf Child in Public Schools: A Handbook for Parents of Deaf Children* (Danville, IL, 1974), 38.

40. Mark Ross, with Diane Brackett and Antonia Maxon, *Hard of Hearing Children in Regular Schools* (Englewood Cliffs, NJ, 1982), 48–49.

41. Thomas S. Spradley and James P. Spradley, *Deaf Like Me* (Washington, DC, 1978), 200–25, 279.

42. Spradley and Spradley, *Deaf Like Me*, 279–81. Two other provocative and revealing narratives on deafness during this period include Paul West, *Words for a Deaf Daughter* (New York, 1968), a nearly poetic and deeply personal response of a hearing father to the challenges faced by his deaf daughter; and Lou Ann Walker, *A Loss for Words: The Story of Deafness in a Family* (New York, 1986), written by a hearing child living with deaf parents.

43. Berthold Lowenfeld, ed., *The Visually Handicapped Child in School* (New York, 1973), 17–24; Hendrickson, *From Shelter to Self-Reliance*, 178–80; Berthold Lowenfeld, *Our Blind Children: Growing and Learning with Them*, 2nd ed. (Springfield, IL, 1964), 136–61.

44. Hendrickson, *From Shelter to Self-Reliance*, 180; Lowenfeld, *Our Blind Children*, 149–53; the quote on segregated class is from Georgie Lee Abel and appears in Lowenfeld, *Our Blind Children*, 157–58.

45. Sherry Raynor and Richard Drouillard, *Get a Wiggle On: A Guide for Helping Visually Impaired Children Grow* (Mason, MI, 1975), 3–11.

46. Eileen P. Scott, James E. Jan, and Roger D. Freeman, *Can't Your Child See?* (Baltimore, MD, 1977), 166–68.

47. James Haskins, with J. M. Stifle, *The Quiet Revolution: The Struggle for the Rights of Disabled Americans* (New York, 1979), 41–51.

48. Douglas Biklen, "Exclusion," *Peabody Journal of Education* 50 (April 1973): 226–34; quote is from 234. See also Helen Featherstone, *A Difference in the Family: Life with a Disabled Child* (New York, 1980); Lotte E. Moise, "Will the Real Advocate for Retarded Persons Please Stand Up!" Reprinted from *Child Welfare*, January 1975, ARC Files, Drawer E; and Ray H. Barsch, *The Parent of the Handicapped Child: The Study of Child-rearing Practices* (Springfield, IL, 1968), 218–25.

6

Voices of the Present, Echoes from the Past: Considering the Lives of Children with Disabilities

Since the early 1980s, public policy toward children with disabilities has undergone a remarkable and significant transformation. The reauthorization and subsequent revisions of the original PL 94-142, now known as the Individuals with Disabilities Education Act (IDEA), have greatly extended the reach of guaranteed services to disabled children from birth to age 21. There also have been added several new categories of disability, including Traumatic Brain Injury, Autism, and Attention Deficit–Hyperactivity Disorder (covered under several possible health- or behavior-related categories). The Americans with Disabilities Act (ADA) of 1990 addressed concerns for persons with disabilities of all ages regarding accommodations to disability in all walks of life and work. As a result, today the American public has a greater awareness of issues related to disability and how they affect the lives of children than it did even a generation ago.

Yet in many ways little has changed for children with disabilities since the mid-1800s, at least in terms of the way they perceive and are perceived by American society. In this book we have been exploring the lived experiences of children with disabilities who have been shaped by a world that has offered them a multitude of contradictory messages. The history of childhood disabilities is remarkably consistent: parents, teachers, and even students continue to express concerns and viewpoints that were stated either directly or indirectly

150 years ago. Consider the following recent quotes from parents and students involved in special education:

> When kids with special needs were first given the opportunity to go to school, they were separated. That's how it was done because that's what we thought was best. Now we know that it's better for kids with and without disabilities to grow up and learn alongside one another. We need to start out when they are young so that these kids, when they are our community leaders, will accept people who are different and give them the opportunities to succeed that everyone deserves. [Parent of a child with special needs, 1996][1]

> I do not want the "retarded corner" of the school. [special education student, 1994][2]

> I have experienced both, mainstream and deaf school. I'm not disabled, just deaf. Learning through an interpreter is very hard; it's bad socially in the mainstream; you are always outnumbered; you don't feel like it's your school; you never know deaf adults; you don't belong; you don't feel comfortable as a deaf person. [Deaf student in a regular classroom, 1992][3]

Embedded in these words are themes, concerns, and possibilities about the lives of children with disabilities that have existed since the beginning of special education in the United States. Those persons involved in the early years of formal education for disabled youngsters experienced much the same kind of hope, frustration, alienation, and uncertain identity expressed above. This chapter offers some reflections on the assumptions and beliefs about childhood and disability that reflect this continuity in the history of the lived experiences of children with disabilities in this country. Indeed, the questions and themes noted in the Introduction speak to these reflections in multiple ways.

THE PRACTICALITY OF SPECIAL EDUCATION: EFFICIENCY IN SCHOOL OPERATION Vs. THE NEEDS OF CHILDREN

In the decade immediately following the passage of PL 94-142 in 1975, participants and stakeholders in special education encountered a series of obstacles as well as pleasant surprises on the road to more thorough and authentic mainstreaming of children with disabilities in the public schools. Experiences and judgments varied drastically as to the value and efficacy of the mainstreaming movement. Witness these two summations of the impact of the law, published less than two years apart:

> Initially, laws promising education for handicapped children appear as a human effort on the part of our government to embody in legislation the basic Constitutional guarantee of equal opportunity for all. In reality, PL 94-142 is an ill-conceived law embodying a "Pollyanna-Horatio-Alger-like euphoria contrary to fact perception of reality." It threatens the education of an entire generation of handicapped youth and squanders the limited educational funds available in our country for both disabled and regular children. . . . At a practical level, PL 94-142 jeopardizes realistic efforts at serving disabled children by legislating the impossible and by indiscriminately wasting fiscal resources. . . .
>
> If the road to hell is paved with good intentions, PL 94-142 certainly represents enough of a brick to cover half the distance. It is to education what Three Mile Island is to the use of nuclear energy. [1981]

> Does mainstreaming work? It clearly does. . . . Change is never easy, but in our travels we have seen remarkable progress. Parents who once took what they could beg now actively monitor the quality of the education their disabled children receive. Children once sentenced to the wards of huge institutions now sit side by side with high-achieving youngsters in high-prestige schools. Everywhere people are speaking a different language, becoming sensitive to the derogatory connotations of such words as "cripple" and "retard," understanding disabled students as people endowed with human rights. We have seen teachers and principals flourish under the challenge of doing things differently for youngsters who are different.
>
> . . . [Any] supposed failures of mainstreaming are problems of organizational arrangements, internecine politics, and a lack of will and skill of school personnel. [1983][4]

These viewpoints represent not only differences of opinion but also of perspective and priorities. Disagreements regarding the structure, operation, and value systems of education for students with disabilities have existed since such programs began. On the one hand are arguments that focus on the impact of special education on the structures, budgets, and operation of schools and school systems. On the other hand are those that claim the only concern should be the effective education and socialization of the children assigned to special education and, additionally, its impact on *all* children. Such arguments exist in varying degrees along a continuum, of course, and by no means fall into an either–or positioning. Yet the differences are real and significant. As special education has entered the current era, stakeholders in special education have become more vocal about these issues, with their views reaching a much wider—and perhaps more attentive—audience than ever before.

Originally, special education in the public schools addressed the perceived needs of the teachers and the schools more than those of students considered eligible for it. Teachers in the 1800s faced enormous class sizes by today's standards—often as many as seventy or eighty in some of the large urban systems. Teachers worried the most about pupils whose academic struggles and behavioral problems created numerous distractions. As early as the 1850s, teachers in Boston called attention to such children, pleading for their removal from the classroom in order to make their workload more manageable and their teaching more efficient. Moreover, the rapidly growing urban school systems grew increasingly concerned over students whose struggles led to their "lagging" in the regular classroom. Such students seemed to interfere with the efficient operation of schooling by failing to keep pace in moving up the educational ladder. Their removal to a specialized setting where they could be isolated from the proper flow of students pleased frustrated teachers as well as efficiency-minded administrators. Even settings such as the Horace Mann School for the Deaf in Boston, which clearly targeted a specific population for instructional purposes, was founded largely to save money: it was cheaper for the city to operate a day school for resident deaf children than to help fund their education and residency at a distant state institution.[5]

In some respects, children in public school special education were viewed the same as were all students: as units to be managed effectively and prepared to be functioning members of society. At least for most school administrators, the pressures of rapidly growing urban school systems filled with children from a wide range of ethnic and linguistic backgrounds left little time and few resources for caring too much about any individual child. In small-town and rural districts, children with disabilities—typically not formally identified, at least until the 1940s—attended and participated in normal school activities to the extent they could. Teachers adjusted instruction accordingly. Disabled children neither demanded nor obtained more special treatment than any other child, at least until such districts developed special education programs. To public school officials, children with disabilities were by and large students first and exceptional students second, at least until the mid–twentieth century.

Nevertheless, there also have always been teachers and administrators who focused their attention on disabled students and sought to bring a truly *special* education to them. While certainly a distinct (almost invisible) minority in the early period of special education, their ranks increased steadily as special education programs expanded, specialized teacher training for students with disabilities became entrenched, and special educators found that their time with the children themselves enriched their professional lives. Even among the earliest special education teachers—for example, Harriet Lyman and the staff at the Horace Mann School in Boston and Elizabeth Farrell in the special classes of New York City—one could see in their writings an intimate connection with their students. These educators, assisted by small class size, recognized the uniqueness of their pupils and established a personal relationship with them. Among these educators there was a commitment to giving each child a chance to succeed on her or his own terms.

These distinctions between the needs of the schools and the needs of disabled pupils exist even today. Many of the debates circulating around the concept of inclusion focus less on the children and more on the ideology, legal issues, or practical ramifications involved. At the heart of much of this discussion lies the issue of money: to what extent is special education defined, or even driven, by financial considerations? To what extent are these children "worth it"? How much is too much for a district in making "reasonable accommodations" for a disabled child, according to law? McCay Vernon, a strong early critic of PL 94-142, openly challenged spending $60,000 a year on "Judy," a "psychotic child three years old ... [who] is severely mentally retarded and has multiple other physical and psychological problems." Using Judy as an example, Vernon asks bluntly whether "we as a country [should] be making by far our heaviest per capita educational financial investments in those youths least able to contribute to society."[6] Furthermore, the debate over the funding of special education and the practice of making decisions based on either cost to, or in many instances potential income for, the school clearly shows that the children involved are by no means the top priority. Others suggest that cost should never be an issue, that a child is a child and worth whatever the price to accommodate them successfully in the public schools. Multiple court cases involving children with disabilities have considered this very question. Efficiency and cost have been fundamental issues in special education since its inception; in many such instances the central concerns of children themselves have taken a back seat.[7]

ISOLATION, REJECTION, AND ACCEPTANCE: THE LIVES OF CHILDREN IN SCHOOLS AND INSTITUTIONS

Such monetary considerations were of little direct concern to the students in special education. For them, the realities of the classroom and of their place in school took center stage in their lives. For most of these children, the typical school day resembled that of all other students: routine, predictable activities planned by teachers. The nature of these activities depended on the particular setting, which in turn usually depended on the nature of the disability being addressed and the age of the children involved. There exists no evidence that special education classes lasted shorter or longer than the standard school day. The quality of teaching in special education classrooms likely varied as much as it did in regular classrooms (although in its early stages—especially before formal training programs for special educators took hold—teachers who were struggling in a regular classroom might well have been reassigned to a "special" classroom). As special education teachers developed better skills and a stronger sense of collegiality and purpose, the quality of instruction probably improved. For the students, a standard fare mixing academic, practical, and vocational content in varying degrees was the norm.[8]

What was different for these children was their segregation from their "normal" peers. Many thousands of students with speech disorders or other noncognitive or nonbehavioral conditions received a few hours each week in special training but then spent the rest of their time in a regular classroom. However, most children formally identified as disabled experienced complete and permanent separation from their nondisabled schoolmates from the 1850s until well into the 1970s. Disabled children attended separate classes in isolated classrooms or even special schools—for example, those for "crippled" children. Segregation presumably promoted school efficiency, protected the disabled and nondisabled from each other, and enabled greater personal attention and more appropriate and effective instruction for all students regardless of label. It also created chasms between children, generating mutual suspicion, ridicule, and a serious lack of compassion and understanding. The debate over the merits and drawbacks of segregated special education, which began in earnest as early as the 1940s, continues in full force to this day.

For children living in residential institutions, life truly existed outside the mainstream of society. As noted in an earlier chapter, the nature of life inside the institutions for the mentally disabled remained a mystery to the public for generations. Annual reports of superintendents, members of boards of oversight, or government officials revealed only a sanitized view of institutional life. Even as the public perception of the capabilities of institutionalized mentally disabled children grew increasingly pessimistic in the late 1800s, official reports from these institutions proclaimed them to be efficient, humane, and effective vehicles for social control. However, the photographic and narrative exposés of the mid-1900s as well as recent scholarship has opened up a world that was at once disturbing and heartbreaking. Children engaged in aimless activity, or did nothing at all. They lived in hellish conditions. Attendants appeared incompetent and uncaring. Images of seriously disabled children living in various states of environmental and psychological despair startled the public and helped catalyze the deinstitutionalization and normalization movements of the early 1970s.

Children in residential institutions for the deaf and for the blind apparently fared much better. These institutions avoided becoming warehouses for children abandoned by society. They sustained their strong educational purpose and function for a small but capable student population. The relative clarity of the disabilities and the specific nature of instructional techniques for the blind and for the deaf further solidified the reputations of these institutions. Even the intense debate within the deaf community regarding the merits of oralism versus manualism did not destroy institutions for the deaf. Dedicated teachers and staff, most of whom had considerable training in the treatment of deafness or blindness and in the effective education of children with these conditions, contributed to the reputation of these institutions. Consequently, conditions within these institutions were significantly better than those in institutions for the mentally disabled. The children within benefited accordingly.

THE LIVES OF DISABLED CHILDREN: THROUGH THE EYES OF PARENTS

Parental involvement in the lives of children with disabilities has always been hugely important. Given the limited body of historical evidence produced by children with disabilities themselves regarding their lives, much of what is known about those lives comes from the words and actions of parents. Unfortunately, their voices have not revealed much at least until recently. During the nineteenth century, civic and educational leaders did not see parents as partners or allies in efforts to address disability. Most parents of children with obvious and/or serious disabilities kept their child at home, sequestered from the skeptical eyes of neighbors and strangers. Those whose children did attend schools or reside in institutions usually were quietly deferential to the advice and directives of professionals or doctors. State agencies were often hostile to parents of disabled children, who were labeled unreliable and became the targets of legislation and policies that attempted to compensate for parents' alleged lack of concern or cooperation regarding the child's activities and behavior. As belief in the hereditary nature of mental disability gained credence between the late nineteenth century and the early twentieth century, parents were widely believed to be responsible for perpetuating disability through procreation and thus became highly suspect, if not contemptible, in the eyes of the public.

As public schools became more involved in the lives of disabled children, parents gradually came to be seen as allies and partners in addressing issues and conditions of disability. Social workers sought to enlist the entire family to assist in correcting social pathologies associated with disability. Parents often resisted placement of their child in special education; they believed that it was either too stigmatizing or that their child did not need it. However, most parents complied eventually. Parents did not understand disability as did school personnel and social workers. But parents also spent a great deal of time with their disabled children, and professionals sought to enlist them as allies in their attempts to keep disability manageable and under control in the community.

Parents of mentally disabled children struggled to understand the nature, extent, and impact of their child's condition. The severity of the disability significantly affected the family's home and school life, as caring for a significantly disabled child typically required an unusual amount of energy and patience. Parents of any obviously disabled child had to cope with social assumptions and prejudices concerning the origins and manifestations of the disabling condition. Life in homes affected by significant disability thus presented serious challenges regardless of the socioeconomic status of the family. Even for children with mild disabilities, segregation in school often generated an acute awareness of being different on the part of the child, which may well have carried over into the child's home and social life.

After World War II, however, the voices of parents grew much stronger. Parent groups had formed locally and informally as early as the late 1930s in an effort to help parents find solace and solutions regarding their multiple struggles with their disabled children. In response to parents' expressed interest, this advice often appeared in the popular press instead of the professional literature and addressed practical as well as general concerns about their child's welfare. Parents became more knowledgeable about disability and more activist in their approach to addressing it. Their conflicts with professionals reflect these shifts in power and authority. Nevertheless, parents in the 1960s and 1970s still took second billing to medical, psychological, and educational professionals in terms of determining what was "best" for their child. The angst and frustration expressed by so many parents who were advised "put him away" or "don't become attached" or "let's just see if it goes away" reflected their still secondary position vis-à-vis professionals in the field. Theirs was often a painful yet instructive learning process. As one parent noted, "It seems as if our son is constantly being tested. I know they have to know where he stands so they will know what to work on, but sometimes it seems as if they do more testing than teaching." Another parent spoke to the inconsistent effort of professionals who worked with her child (a problem special needs children of course shared with all students): "I've discovered that how much our daughter learns is directly related to the quality of the professionals who are teaching her. Some of them are so much more knowledgeable and skilled at getting and keeping our daughter's interest in the task at hand. Others of them seem kind of burnt out or apathetic." Meanwhile, more and more parents spoke about their trials, sorrows, and joys at home with a disabled child—at first to each other, then to the doctors and teachers, and eventually to the public at large.[9]

As parents spoke out more, the lives of children with disabilities became more readily discernible. The first few years after the passage of PL 94-142 represented a new and challenging era of parental involvement in disability and the ways in which it affected children. After the law's enactment, many parents learned that they needed to advocate strongly and persistently for the rights of their disabled children in order to get schools, government, the judiciary, and the public truly engaged in ensuring those rights and implementing the provisions of the law. Such activism occurred on several fronts. At the school level, parents slowly assumed more of a role in developing the Individualized Education Plans mandated by PL 94-142. Parents who believed they had failed in securing their child's rights resorted to legal action more often than in the pre-1975 era. These lawsuits in turn contributed to a growing corpus of legal decisions addressing the question of the extent to which school districts were expected to adapt facilities and instruction to accommodate children with disabilities. Parents also became more involved in advocacy and professional groups such as The Arc, The Association for Students with Severe Handicaps (TASH), the Council for Exceptional Children (CEC), Children and Adults with Attention-Deficit/Hyperactivity Disorder (CHADD), and the Learning Disabilities Association of America (LDA). One highly visible example of how parents became much more actively involved in the political and legal processes of fighting for the rights of their children with disabilities occurred in Richmond, California, in the early 1980s. In this case, parents took active leadership roles in challenging school regulations and lobbying the government, in order to secure what they felt was a more appropriate and effective public education for their children.[10]

IDEOLOGY, ETHICS, AND THE DIGNITY OF PERSONS WITH DISABILITIES: AN EYE TO THE FUTURE

The signal feature of the lives of children considered disabled has been their marginalization from other children and the rest of society. Ironically, children who today might well be identified as mildly disabled—whether cognitively, physically, or behaviorally—often escaped such labels at least until the early twentieth century. Indeed, the absence of "sophisticated" mechanisms for "finding" disability, and the fact that children found their "subnormal" abilities had little bearing on their ability to function as a member of their family and small community, rendered such mild forms of disability either invisible or insignificant. However, until the early twentieth century, those children whose disabilities were obvious and/or debilitating were typically hidden away in homes, residential institutions for the disabled, or public facilities for the impoverished. Once public schools began to enroll more and more children with identifiable disabilities, severely disabled children found themselves in separate settings where they had little if any interaction with "normal" students. Even as segregation of disabled children began to crumble in the 1970s, they still had to struggle to gain authentic participation in school and community life. The stigma of disability and the continued limited access to standard public facilities and activities keep a large number of children with disabilities on the outside looking in. As one student expressed it,

> Summing it up, the only contact we had with the "normal" children was visual. We stared at each other. On those occasions, I can report my own feelings: embarrassment. Given the loud, clear message that was daily being delivered to them, I feel quite confident that I can also report their feelings: YECH! . . . We were in school because children go to school but we were outcasts, with no future and no expectations of one.[11]

Advocates for disabled youngsters identified this marginalization as a key societal flaw and attacked it accordingly. Deliberate integration in schools and communities constituted their primary weapon. With the full force of the law behind them, advocates—as well as many persons with disabilities themselves—challenged society to reconsider traditions of segregation, marginalization, and degradation of the disabled. Deinstitutionalization, mainstreaming, access, accommodation, and equity became rallying cries for those committed to improving the quality of life for disabled children and their families. "[The] democratic ideals of American society can best be served and protected when diversity is highly valued and seen as the norm in all schools," voiced The Association for Persons with Severe Handicaps. "[TASH] reaffirms that students with disabilities belong in general education classrooms and that they receive the supports and services necessary to benefit from their education in the general education setting."[12]

Regrettably, such efforts have met considerable resistance on a number of fronts. Children with disabilities have been subjects of scorn, rumor, paternalism, condescension, and even of sympathy and compassion. They have been the subjects of experimental social policies toward disability. Over time their lives have raised more questions about *what* they are than *who* they are. Those with mild or less obvious disabilities still were often avoided in the community; typically segregated from their nondisabled peers at school; frequently subjected to a range of tests, school programs, or other interventions designed to render them more functional in school or the workplace and hence more useful to society; and at times singled out as incompetent, annoying, or even dangerous. In 1993, the American Federation of Teachers expressed grave concern about the placement of disabled children in regular classrooms "regardless of the nature or severity of their disabilities, their ability to behave or function appropriately in the classroom, or the educational benefits they and their peers can derive."[13] For children with more severe cases of cognitive or behavioral disability, life could take an unmistakably dark turn: institutionalized, isolated, abused, and denied of their basic rights, rejected by families and neighbors, treated as little more than animal-like subjects by researchers, doctors, or other professionals. Although those in the latter category constituted only a small minority of children who have been identified as disabled, the lives they have led have represented a much more shameful and indefensible aspect of the treatment of disability in American society.

Yet during the past thirty years, a remarkable series of individualized and collective, limited and comprehensive, as well as practice- and ethics-based efforts to improve the lives of all children with disabilities have occurred. These have focused on a wide range of social institutions. Schools, community service agencies, families, employers, health care facilities, and faith-based organizations have all been called upon to support children identified as disabled and enhance the quality of services provided to them. Such efforts have addressed broad concerns such as access, financial resources, equitable treatment, and validation through dignity and respect. As John Dewey might have phrased it, the ultimate goal of this movement may well be said to render the immediate world of the child—the only world the child knows, whether or not she or he is aware of how that world is seen by others—more agreeable, more worthwhile, and more valued. Certainly, these efforts must confront and wrestle with a centuries-long legacy of ambivalence, neglect, misconceptions, and intentional attacks on the nature and character of persons identified as disabled. Furthermore there still exists significant disagreement as to what constitutes the best paths of action for enriching and validating their lives. Indeed, this complex, often contradictory legacy may well complicate or slow the success of efforts to improve the quality of life for children with disabilities. However, recent trends and initiatives—far more sizable in terms of number, strength, and commitment than similar efforts in the past—strongly suggest that an important corner has been turned. Let us hope that we continue to move toward an era of dignity and equity, and that there will be no turning back.

NOTES

1. Kathy Martin, in National Council on Disability, *Achieving Independence: The Challenge for the 21st Century: A Decade of Progress in Disability Policy; Setting an Agenda for the Future* (Washington, DC, 1996), 44–45.

2. Linda Preston, in President's Committee on Mental Retardation, *Report to the President: The National Reform Agenda and Citizens with Mental Retardation; A Journey of Renewal for All Americans* (Washington, DC, 1994), 6.

3. Jesse Thomas, in Harlan Lane, *The Mask of Benevolence: Disabling the Deaf Community* (New York, 1992), 136.

4. McCay Vernon, "Education's 'Three Mile Island': PL 94-142," *Peabody Journal of Education* 59 (1981/1982): 24, 29; Robert Bogdan, "'Does Mainstreaming Work?' Is a Silly Question," *Phi Delta Kappan* 64 (February 1983): 428.

5. Robert L. Osgood, *For "Children Who Vary from the Normal Type": Special Education in Boston 1838–1930* (Washington, DC, 2000), 72–78, 93–95.

6. Vernon, "Education's 'Three Mile Island,'" 27.

7. Nikki Murdick, Barbara Gartin, and Terry Crabtree, *Special Education Law* (Upper Saddle River, NJ, 2002), 95–111.

8. Osgood, *For "Children Who Vary from the Normal Type,"* 85–89.

9. Quoted in M. Cay Holbrook, *Children with Visual Impairments: A Parents' Guide* (Bethesda, MD, 1996), 203–4.

10. Julia Landau, "The Richmond Case Study: Ending Segregated Education for Disabled Children," in *Stepping Stones: Successful Advocacy for Children*, ed. Sheryl Dicker (New York, 1990), 113–56.

11. Quoted in Massachusetts Advocacy Center, *Out of the Mainstream: Education of Disabled Youth in Massachusetts* (Boston, MA, 1987), 4.

12. The Association for Persons with Severe Handicaps, "Resolution on Inclusive Education," reprinted in James M. Kauffman and Daniel P. Hallahan, eds., *The Illusion of Full Inclusion: A Comprehensive Critique of a Current Special Education Bandwagon* (Austin, TX, 1995), 314.

13. American Federation of Teachers, "American Federation of Teachers Resolution: Inclusion of Students with Disabilities," in ibid., 312.

Bibliography

BOOKS AND PAMPHLETS

Anderson, Meta. *Education of Defectives in the Public Schools.* Yonkers-on-Hudson, NY: World Book, 1917.

Antin, Mary. *The Promised Land.* Boston: Houghton Mifflin, 1912.

Ashby, LeRoy. *Endangered Children: Dependency, Neglect, and Abuse in American History.* New York: Twayne, 1997.

———. *Saving the Waifs: Reformers and Dependent Children, 1890–1917.* Philadelphia, PA: Temple University Press, 1984.

Barnartt, Sharon, and Richard Scotch. *Disability Protests: Contentious Politics 1970–1999.* Washington, DC: Gallaudet University Press, 2001.

Barsch, Ray H. *The Parent of the Handicapped Child: The Study of Child-rearing Practices.* Springfield, IL: Charles C. Thomas, 1968.

Baynton, Douglas. *Forbidden Signs: American Culture and the Campaign against Sign Language.* Chicago, IL: University of Chicago Press, 1996.

Beatty, Barbara, Emily D. Cahan, and Julia Grant, eds. *When Science Encounters the Child: Education, Parenting, and Child Welfare in 20th-Century America.* New York: Teachers College Press, 2006.

Berrol, Selma. *Growing Up American: Immigrant Children in America, Then and Now.* New York: Twayne, 1995.

Best, Harry. *Blindness and the Blind in the United States.* New York: Macmillan, 1934.

———. *Deafness and the Deaf in the United States: Considered Primarily in Relation to Those Sometimes More or Less Erroneously Known as "Deaf-Mutes."* New York: Macmillan, 1943.

Blatt, Burton, and Fred Kaplan. *Christmas in Purgatory: A Photographic Essay on Mental Retardation.* Boston, MA: Allyn and Bacon, 1966.

Brutten, Milton, Sylvia O. Richardson, and Charles Mangel. *Something's Wrong with My Child: A Parents' Book about Children with Learning Disabilities*. New York: Harcourt Brace Jovanovich, 1973.

Buck, Pearl. *The Child Who Never Grew*. New York: John Day and Co., 1950.

Burton, Warren. *The District School as It Was by One Who Went to It*. New York: Arno Press, 1928.

Centerwall, Siegried A., and Willard R. Centerwall. *Mental Retardation*. Loma Linda, CA: Loma Linda University, 1961. ARC Files, Drawer E.

Clement, Priscilla Ferguson. *Growing Pains: Children in the Industrial Age, 1850–1890*. New York: Twayne, 1997.

Cremin, Lawrence. *American Education: The National Experience 1783–1976*. New York: Harper and Row, 1980.

———. *The Transformation of the School: Progressivism in American Education 1876–1957*. New York: Vintage, 1964.

D'Antonio, Michael. *The State Boys Rebellion*. New York: Simon and Schuster, 2004.

Davies, Stanley Powell. *Social Control of the Mentally Deficient*. New York: Thomas Y. Crowell, 1930.

Davis, Lenwood G., ed. *A History of Urban Growth and Development: A Selected Bibliography of Published Works on the History of Urban Growth and Development in the United States, 1872–1972*. Monticello, IL: Council of Planning Librarians,1972.

Deutsch, Albert. *The Mentally Ill in America: A History of Their Care and Treatment from Colonial Times*. New York: Columbia University Press, 1949.

———. *The Shame of the States*. New York: Harcourt, Brace, 1948.

Dewey, John. *The School and Society / The Child and the Curriculum*. Chicago, IL: University of Chicago Press, 1990.

DiMichael, Salvatore G. "The Mentally Retarded Child in Home and Community". New York: NARC, n.d. ARC Files, Drawer C.

Dugdale, R. L. *The Jukes: A Study in Crime, Pauperism, Disease and Heredity*. New York: G. P. Putnam, 1877.

Ecob, Katharine G. *Deciding What's Best for Your Retarded Child*. New York: NARC, 1959. ARC Files, Drawer B.

Eggleston, Edward. *The Hoosier Schoolmaster*. Bloomington, IN: Indiana University Press, 1984.

Elliott, Maude Howe. *Laura Bridgman: Dr. Howe's Famous Pupil and What He Taught Her*. Boston, MA: Little, Brown, 1903.

Emerson, Ralph Waldo. *The Political Emerson: Essential Writings on Politics and Social Reform*. Boston, MA: Beacon Press, 2004.

Featherstone, Helen. *A Difference in the Family: Life with a Disabled Child*. New York: Basic Books, 1980.

Filler, Louis. *Abolition and Social Justice in the Era of Reform*. New York: Harper and Row, 1972.

Flanagan, Maureen A. *Progressives and Progressivisms: 1890s–1920s*. New York: Oxford University Press, 2007.

Fleischer, Doris Zames, and Freida Zames. *The Disability Rights Movement: From Charity to Confrontation*. Philadelphia, PA: Temple University Press, 2001.

Foster, Harriet McIntyre. *The Education of Idiots and Imbeciles. A Paper Read Before the Social Science Association of Indiana*. Indianapolis, IN: Indianapolis Journal Co., 1879.

Frampton, Merle F., and Ellen Kerney. *The Residential School: Its History, Contributions, and Future*. New York: New York Institute for the Education of the Blind, 1953.

Franklin, Barry M. *From "Backwardness" to "At-Risk": Childhood Learning Difficulties and the Contradictions of School Reform*. Albany, NY: SUNY Press, 1994.

Fraser, Stewart E., and William W. Brickman, eds. *A History of International and Comparative Education: Nineteenth-Century Documents*. Glenview, IL: Scott Forsman, 1968.

Freeberg, Ernest. *The Education of Laura Bridgman: First Deaf and Blind Person to Learn Language*. Cambridge, MA: Harvard University Press, 2001.

Gitter, Elisabeth. *The Imprisoned Guest: Samuel Howe and Laura Bridgman, the Original Deaf-Blind Girl*. New York: Farrar, Straus and Giroux, 2001.

Goddard, Henry Herbert. *The Kallikak Family: A Study in the Heredity of Feeblemindedness*. New York: Macmillan, 1912.

Grannon, Bernice. *A Letter to Parents*. New York: National Association of Retarded Children, 1954.

Grob, Gerald. *Mental Illness and American Society, 1875–1940*. Princeton, NJ: Princeton University Press, 1983.

Gutek, Gerald L. *A History of the Western Educational Experience*. Prospect Heights, IL: Waveland Press, 1972.

Hallahan, Daniel P., and James M. Kauffman. *Exceptional Children: Introduction to Special Education*, 4th ed. Englewood Cliffs, NJ: Prentice Hall, 1988.

Handlin, Oscar. *Boston's Immigrants: A Study in Acculturation*. Cambridge, MA: Harvard University Press, 1979.

———. *The Uprooted*. Boston: Little, Brown, 1973.

Haskins, James, and J. M. Stifle. *The Quiet Revolution: The Struggle for the Rights of Disabled Americans*. New York: Crowell, 1979.

Heilbroner, Robert L. *The Economic Transformation of America: 1600 to the Present*. Fort Worth, TX: Harcourt Brace College Publishers, 1994.

Hendrickson, Walter B. *From Shelter to Self-Reliance: A History of the Illinois Braille and Sight-Saving School*. Jacksonville, IL: Illinois Braille and Sight-Saving School, 1972.

Higham, John. *Strangers in the Land: Patterns of American Nativism*. New Brunswick, NJ: Rutgers University Press, 1955.

Hindman, Hugh D. *Child Labor: An American History*. Armonk, NY: M. E. Sharpe, 2002.

Holbrook, M. Cay. *Children with Visual Impairments: A Parents' Guide*. Bethesda, MD: Woodbine House, 1996.

Husband, Julie. *Daily Life in the Industrial United States, 1870–1900*. Westport, CT: Greenwood Press, 2004.

Illick, Joseph E. *American Childhoods*. Philadelphia, PA: University of Pennsylvania Press, 2002.

Johnson, Alexander. *Adventures in Social Welfare: Being Reminiscences of Things, Thoughts, and Folks During Forty Years in Social Work*. Fort Wayne, IN: Author, 1923.

Kaestle, Carl F. *Pillars of the Republic: Common Schools and American Society, 1780–1860*. New York: Hill and Wang, 1983.

Kanner, Leo. *A History of the Care and Study of the Mentally Retarded*. Springfield, IL: Charles Thomas, 1964.

Katz, Lee, Steve L. Mathis III, and Edward C. Merrill Jr. *The Deaf Child in Public Schools: A Handbook for Parents of Deaf Children*. Danville, IL: Interstate Publishers and Printers, 1974.

Katz, Michael B. *The Irony of Early School Reform: Educational Innovation in Mid-Nineteenth Century Massachusetts*. Boston, MA: Beacon Press, 1968.

———. *Class, Bureaucracy, and Schools: The Illusion of Educational Change in America*. New York: Praeger, 1975.

Katz, Michael S. *A History of Compulsory Education Laws*. Bloomington, IN: Phi Delta Kappa, 1976.

Kauffman, James M., and Daniel P. Hallahan, eds. *The Illusion of Full Inclusion: A Comprehensive Critique of a Current Special Education Bandwagon*. Austin, TX: Pro-Ed, 1995.

Kaufman, Polly Welts, ed. *Women Teachers on the Frontier*. New Haven, CT: Yale University Press, 1984.

Keller, Helen. *The Story of My Life*. New York: Doubleday, Page, and Co., 1903.

Kliebard, Herbert M. *The Struggle for the American Curriculum, 1893–1958*, 3rd ed. New York: Routledge Falmer, 2004.

Lane, Harlan. *The Mask of Benevolence: Disabling the Deaf Community*. New York: Knopf, 1992.

Latimer, Henry Randolph. *The Conquest of Blindness: An Autobiographical Review of the Life and Work of Henry Randolph Latimer*. New York: American Foundation for the Blind, 1937.

Laurie, Bruce. *Beyond Garrison: Antislavery and Social Reform*. Cambridge, UK: Cambridge University Press, 2005.

Lazerson, Marvin. *Origins of the Urban School: Public Education in Massachusetts, 1870–1915*. Cambridge, MA: Harvard University Press, 1971.

Levine, Erwin L., and Elizabeth M. Wexler. *PL 94-142: An Act of Congress*. New York: Macmillan, 1981.

Licht, Walter. *Industrializing America: The Nineteenth Century*. Baltimore, MD: Johns Hopkins University Press, 1995.

Lowenfeld, Berthold. *Our Blind Children: Growing and Learning with Them*, 2nd ed. Springfield, IL: Charles C. Thomas, 1964.

———, ed. *The Visually Handicapped Child in School*. New York: John Day, 1973.

Mackie, Romaine. *Special Education in the United States: Statistics 1948–1966*. New York: Teachers College Press, 1969.

MacLeod, David. *The Age of the Child: Children in America, 1890–1920*. New York: Twayne, 1998.

McGerr, Michael E. *A Fierce Discontent: The Rise and Fall of the Progressive Movement in America, 1870–1920*. Oxford, UK: Oxford University Press, 2005.

Meyer, David R. *The Roots of American Industrialization*. Baltimore, MD: Johns Hopkins University Press, 2003.

Mintz, Steven. *Huck's Raft: A History of American Childhood*. Cambridge, MA: Harvard University Press, 2004.

———. *Moralists and Modernizers: America's Pre-Civil War Reformers*. Baltimore, MD: Johns Hopkins University Press, 1995.

Monroe, Paul. *Founding of the American Public School System*. Vol. 1. New York: Hafner, 1940.

Murdick, Nikki, Barbara Gartin, and Terry Crabtree. *Special Education Law.* Upper Saddle River, NJ: Merrill Prentice Hall, 2002.

NARC Guardianship Committee. *What Will Happen to My Child? Some Suggestions for Parents Who Are Concerned with Providing Lifetime Protection for a Retarded Son or Daughter.* New York: NARC, 1961.

Nasaw, David. *Children of the City: At Work and at Play.* New York: Oxford University Press, 1985.

National Association for Retarded Children. *The ABC's of Quackery and Sound Medical Care: A Guide for Parents of the Mentally Retarded.* New York: NARC, 1968. ARC Files, Drawer D;

———. "The Mentally Retarded ... Their New Hope." n.d. ARC Files, Drawer C.

———. *Windows of Understanding: A Reading List for Parents Who Are Newly Facing the Discovery of Mental Retardation in Their Child.* New York: NARC, 1959. ARC Files, Drawer E.

Nevins, Allan, and Henry Steele Commager. *A Pocket History of the United States.* New York: Washington Square Press, 1981.

Nielsen, Kim E. *The Radical Lives of Helen Keller.* New York: New York University Press, 2004.

Osgood, Robert L. *For "Children Who Vary from the Normal Type": Special Education in Boston 1838–1930.* Washington, DC: Gallaudet University Press, 2000.

———. *The History of Inclusion in the United States.* Washington, DC: Gallaudet University Press, 2005.

Perrin, John W. *The History of Compulsory Education in New England.* Meadville, PA: Flood & Vincent, 1896.

Raynor, Sherry, and Richard Drouillard. *Get a Wiggle On: A Guide for Helping Visually Impaired Children Grow.* Mason, MI: American Alliance for Health, Physical Education and Recreation, 1975.

Reese, William J. *The Origins of the American High School.* New Haven, CT: Yale University Press, 1995.

———. *Power and the Promise of School Reform: Grassroots Movements during the Progressive Era.* Boston, MA: Routledge and Kegan Paul, 2002.

Reinier, Jacqueline S. *From Virtue to Character: American Childhood, 1775–1850.* New York: Twayne, 1996.

Richards, Laura Elizabeth Howe. *Laura Bridgman; The Story of an Opened Door.* New York: D. Appleton, 1928.

Rippa, S. Alexander. *Education in a Free Society.* 4th ed. New York: Longman, 1980.

Rogers, Dale Evans. *Angel Unaware.* Westwood, NJ: Fleming H. Revell, 1953.

Ross, Mark, Diane Brackett, and Antonia Maxon. *Hard of Hearing Children in Regular Schools.* Englewood Cliffs, NJ: Prentice Hall, 1982.

Rothman, David J. *Conscience and Convenience: The Asylum and Its Alternatives in Progressive America.* Boston, MA: Little, Brown, 1980.

———. *The Discovery of the Asylum: Social Order and Disorder in the New Republic.* Boston, MA: Little, Brown, 1971.

Rothman, David J., and Sheila M. Rothman. *The Willowbrook Wars: A Decade of Struggle for Social Justice.* New York: Harper and Row, 1984.

Rothstein, Stanley William. *Schooling the Poor: A Social Inquiry into the American Educational Experience.* Westport, CT: Bergin and Garvey, 1994.

Safford, Philip L., and Elizabeth J. Safford. *A History of Childhood and Disability*. New York: Teachers College Press, 1996.

Sanders, Elizabeth. *Roots of Reform: Farmers, Workers, and the American State, 1877–1917*. Chicago, IL: University of Chicago Press, 1999.

Sarason, Seymour, and John Doris. *Educational Handicap, Public Policy, and Social History: A Broadened Perspective on Mental Retardation*. New York: Free Press, 1979.

Scheerenberger, R. C. *A History of Mental Retardation*. Baltimore, MD: Paul Brookes, 1983.

Schultz, Stanley K. *The Culture Factory: Boston Public Schools 1789–1860*. New York: Oxford University Press, 1973.

Scott, Eileen P., James E. Jan, and Roger D. Freeman. *Can't Your Child See?* Baltimore, MD: University Park Press, 1977.

Seguin, Edouard. *Report on Education*. 2nd ed. Milwaukee, WI: Doerflinger, 1880.

Spradley, Thomas S., and James P. Spradley. *Deaf Like Me*. Washington, DC: Gallaudet College Press, 1978.

Spring, Joel. *The American School 1642–2000*. 5th ed. Boston, MA: McGraw Hill, 2001.

Staff of the Training School at Vineland, New Jersey. *Home Care of the Mentally Retarded Child*. Vineland, NJ: Training School at Vineland, 1961.

Stroman, Duane F. *The Disability Rights Movement: From Deinstitutionalization to Self-Determination*. Lanham, MD: University Press of America, 2003.

Switzer, Jacqueline Vaughn. *Disabled Rights: American Disability Policy and the Fight for Equality*. Washington, DC: Georgetown University Press, 2003.

Trent Jr., James W. *Inventing the Feeble Mind: A History of Mental Retardation in the United States*. Berkeley, CA: University of California Press, 1994.

Tyack, David. *The One Best System*. Cambridge, MA: Harvard University Press, 1974.

Ulich, Robert. *Education in Western Culture*. New York: Harcourt, Brace, and World, 1965.

Urban, Wayne J., and Jennings L. Wagoner Jr. *American Education: A History*. 3rd ed. Boston, MA: McGraw Hill, 2004.

Van Cleve, John Vickery, and Barry Crouch. *A Place of Their Own: Creating the Deaf Community in America*. Washington, DC: Gallaudet University Press, 1989.

Walker, Lou Ann. *A Loss for Words: The Story of Deafness in a Family*. New York: Harper and Row, 1986.

Wallin, J. E. Wallace. *The Education of Handicapped Children*. Boston, MA: Houghton Mifflin, 1924.

Ward, David. *Poverty, Ethnicity, and the American City, 1840–1935: Changing Conceptions of the Slum and the Ghetto*. Cambridge, UK: Cambridge University Press, 1989.

Weiss, Bernard J., ed. *American Education and the European Immigrant, 1840–1940*. Urbana, IL: University of Illinois Press, 1982.

West, Paul. *Words for a Deaf Daughter*. New York: Harper and Row, 1968.

Winzer, Margret. *The History of Special Education: From Isolation to Integration*. Washington, DC: Gallaudet University Press, 1993.

Wolfensberger, Wolf. *The Principle of Normalization in Human Services*. Toronto, ON: National Institute on Mental Retardation, 1972.

Youcha, Geraldine. *Minding the Children: Child Care in America from Colonial Times to the Present*. Cambridge, MA: De Capo Press, 1995.

Zinn, Howard. *A People's History of the United States*. New York: Harper and Row, 1980.

lifestyle was still very much alive and significant during the late twentieth century—just as it had been one hundred years earlier.[42]

Children who were blind faced similar differences of opinion regarding the optimum setting for their education and socialization. Once again, the question of whether a residential institution or a day school offered the best opportunities for blind children to learn and to grow dominated much of the discourse during this period. By the mid-1960s many residential institutions for the blind offered opportunities for students to extend their education beyond the walls of the institution. Some joined Boy or Girl Scouts, others attended Sunday Schools and many used community recreational facilities such as parks and swimming pools. Many more children had the opportunity to return home for weekends, holidays, and vacation periods because of advances in modes of transportation. On the other hand, public school services such as day schools or special classes for blind or partially sighted children existed in districts where size and resources could support them, as they had for generations. The use of itinerant teachers—specialists in teaching blind children who were assigned to an entire district, not just one school—expanded public school opportunities for children with vision impairments, especially in terms of one-on-one instruction. They also allowed such children to spend more time in a regular classroom.[43]

Debate continued as to the various academic and social advantages and disadvantages of residential versus public school settings. As earlier, the opportunity to live at home with one's family remained a strong advantage of public day school instruction. The inclusion of blind youngsters in regular nursery schools and kindergartens garnered praise from experts as a sound way to familiarize "normal" children with their blind peers and to accept them more readily. In theory, this effect carried into the regular grades. Even so, some experts commented that attending public school in segregated classes "defeats the very purpose for which [the segregated class] was established.... The segregated class cannot possibly offer to its children the equipment, the variety of experiences, and the supplementary instruction which they would get in a residential school." Special schools for the blind had technology specific to the condition of blindness; specially trained teachers; resources for work in art, music, and language arts; and physical as well as vocational education programs designed specifically for blind children.[44]

Of utmost concern to parents and families was taking advantage of opportunities to socialize their blind children effectively. Such efforts of course started soon after birth and/or after identifying the child as blind or visually impaired.

Deaf persons themselves and their families expressed the same kind of ambivalence and variety of perspectives regarding these issues. From the difficult process of learning that one's child is deaf to making decisions about that child's future, parents often struggled with finding the "right" answers to their questions and concerns. For example, in the book *Deaf Like Me*, Thomas and Louise Spradley recounted an uncomfortable yet highly informative meeting with parents of other deaf children attending the Starr King Exceptional School for children with speech and hearing impairments in Sacramento, California. Discussions of problems with discipline, communication, and academics made it clear that their child, Lynn, not only experienced problems with being deaf but also with just being a child. The Spradleys' involvement with the school's decision to replace a pure oralist approach with one that also included finger-spelling and the use of sign language was particularly revealing of the heated controversy within the deaf community itself, especially among hearing parents of deaf children. Considering all the issues raised at these meetings, they poignantly observed, "Several roads fanned out in front of us. All seemed to hold great risks for Lynn. We fell asleep long after midnight, anxious and troubled about the future." As Lynn reported:

> I wanted to go to Berkeley. My parents didn't want me to go away to school. They wanted me to stay at home and attend a mainstream class at a nearby school. But I wanted more friends and teachers I could communicate with easily. English and math were hard for me to understand, and when I came home I didn't have any friends my age who were deaf. My brother, Bruce, had lots of friends. Sometimes I got frustrated and angry or lost my temper.

When the Starr King School hired Linda Raymond, a deaf teacher who used sign language, she helped convince Lynn's parents to send her to the California School for the Deaf in Berkeley.[41]

In the book's epilogue, Lynn described how their decision to send her to the residential state school—where, as she said, "everyone could sign!"— served as a turning point in her life. "Some of my classmates [at the residential school] remembered going to schools like mine where they were not allowed to sign. We thought that was stupid. We felt lucky we had learned to sign and could discuss things so easily. . . . Deaf people are not dumb. Deaf kids are just as smart as hearing kids. With sign language deaf kids can do anything." Lynn's support of a very traditional yet still controversial approach to deaf education and communication demonstrated that this controversy about learning and

22. Catherine Nutterville, "Equality of Educational Opportunity for the Slow-Learning Pupils in High School," *Journal of Exceptional Children* 7 (January 1941): 134.

23. Mabel R. Farson, "Education of the Handicapped Child for Social Competency," *Journal of Exceptional Children* 6 (January 1940): 138–44, 150;

24. Samuel R. Laycock, "Problems in the Adolescence of Exceptional Children," *Journal of Exceptional Children* 9 (April 1943): 203–7.

25. R.C. Scheerenberger, *A History of Mental Retardation* (Baltimore, 1983): 240–41; Romaine Mackie, *Special Education in the United States: Statistics 1948-1966* (New York, 1969), 41.

26. James Trent Jr., *Inventing the "Feeble Mind": A History of Mental Retardation in the United States* (Berkeley, CA, 1994), 225–26.

27. Trent, *Inventing the "Feeble Mind,"* 226–27.

28. Albert Deutsch, *The Shame of the States* (New York, 1948), 132–34.

29. Trent, *Inventing the "Feeble Mind,"* 227–30.

30. Michael D'Antonio, *The State Boys Rebellion* (New York, 2004), 45, 48, 104, 277.

31. Pearl Buck, *The Child Who Never Grew* (New York, 1950).

32. Buck, *The Child Who Never Grew*, 7.

33. Buck, *The Child Who Never Grew*, 22–23, 61–62.

34. Dale Evans Rogers, *Angel Unaware* (Westwood, NJ, 1953), 7.

35. Rogers, *Angel Unaware*, 11–16, 19, 52, 63.

36. Osgood, *The History of Inclusion in the United States*, 56–59.

9. Harrison Allen Dobbs, "Children with Defects: A Frame of Reference," *Peabody Journal of Education* 27 (January 1950): 228–36; Harrison Allen Dobbs, "Children with Defects: Steps Forward," *Peabody Journal of Education* 29 (November 1951): 157–65; Harrison Allen Dobbs, "More Certainty in Educating Children with Defects," *Peabody Journal of Education* 30 (September 1952): 66–74; Harrison Allen Dobbs, "Children with Defects: A Philosophical Proposal," *Peabody Journal of Education* 31 (September 1953): 67–77.

10. Ivan K. Garrison, "A Broader Concept of Normalcy," *Journal of Education* 136 (March 1954): 178–81.

11. For a more thorough discussion of the debate regarding the segregation of special education students in the 1940s and 1950s, see Robert L. Osgood, *The History of Inclusion in the United States* (Washington, DC, 2005), 42–54.

12. Josephine C. Foster and Marion L. Mattson, "The Atypical Child in an Average School," *Childhood Education* 17 (November 1940): 124.

13. Gladys Gardner, "The Nursery School Helps a Retarded Child," *Childhood Education* 21 (May 1945): 453–56.

14. Georgiana S. Mendenhall, "The Influence of the Arts on the Lives of Handicapped Children," *Journal of Exceptional Children* 7 (October 1940): 11–18, 33–34.

15. Marjorie B. Hicks, "Teaching Art to Backward Children," *Journal of Exceptional Children* 6 (February 1940): 172–75; Louise Laird, "Teaching a Retarded Group," *Journal of Education* 121 (October 1938): 227–28; Lydia A. Duggins, "Exceptional Children in the Classroom," *Journal of Education* 133 (October 1950): 200–2.

16. O. J. Hill, "Another Beam of Light through the Darkness," *Journal of Exceptional Children* 6 (January 1940): 129–37; Irene Marquis, "Helping the Visually Handicapped," *Journal of Education* 134 (March, April, 1951): 106–7; Virginia M. Axline, "Understanding and Accepting the Child Who Is Blind," *Childhood Education* 30 (May 1954): 427–30.

17. Margaret Williams Radcliffe, "The Hard of Hearing Child in Our Schools," *Childhood Education* 21 (May 1945): 457; Duggins, "Exceptional Children in the Classroom," 201. See also Marjorie P. Sheldon, "Protection of the Crippled Child from Avoidable Strain in School," *Journal of Exceptional Children* 8 (November 1940): 50–56; George Lavos, "Personality and a Physical Defect," *Journal of Exceptional Children* 7 (January 1941): 124–28, 145–46.

18. Henry Hansburg, "The Case of Daniel," *Childhood Education* 22 (September 1945): 37–40.

19. Marion Nesbitt, " . . . When the 'Different' Child Is Accepted," *Childhood Education* 27 (January 1951): 218–19.

20. Charlotte Kwiat, "Teaching In Little Hell," *Journal of Education* 133 (December 1950): 258–59.

21. Walter B. Barbe, "Locating Children With Emotional Problems," *Childhood Education* 30 (November 1953): 127–30; M. LaVinia Warner, "Problems of the Delinquent Girl," *Journal of Exceptional Children* 7 (December 1940): 102–7, 112; P. F. Valentine, "They Blame the Home for Delinquency," *Educational Forum* 11 (March 1947): 285–87; Katharine F. Lenroot, "Delinquency Prevention Through School and Social Agency Coordination," *Educational Forum* 8 (November 1943): 11–15. See also Alma May Stewart, "Personnel Work With the Special School Pupil," *Journal of Exceptional Children* 6 (May 1940): 283–87, 306, for an interesting discussion of how a special school's entire staff involved itself in diagnosis and treatment of boys with behavior disorders in Chicago.

perspective of her infant daughter, Robin, who was born with Down syndrome, a damaged heart, and other multiple complications and who passed away two days before her second birthday. In the book, Robin speaks to God about her time "Down There," representing the Rogerses' strong belief that her life and disabilities reflected God's "Plan" to teach humans about love, compassion, patience, and faith. The book is filled with references to the Rogerses' devout Christianity. Rogers wrote in the foreword that her daughter "came into the world with an appalling handicap" but that she and her husband "learned some great lessons of truth through His tiny messenger."[34]

While the book by design was heavily couched in a childlike innocence and optimism, it nonetheless addressed important issues of families affected by disability. At the outset of the book, Rogers has Robin describe her birth and the cool, distant professional concern of her doctors. Robin says that it was days before they informed Mrs. Rogers of Robin's condition because "they were all dreading the time when they'd have to tell Mommy and Daddy about the bad shape I was in. . . . That's one thing I learned Down There . . . that the doctors are just beginning to discover how much help You [God] are in any situation. They're beginning to talk seriously about 'tender, loving care.' You are getting through to the doctors." Rogers described through Robin's perspective the daily struggles of feeding and the constant suggestions that she be put away: "it was easier to do it quickly, before the child became entrenched in their hearts. . . . Daddy said, 'No! We'll keep her and do all we can for her, and take our chances." The book continued to detail the heartache and sense of guilt felt by Roy and Dale when they went to work and had to leave Robin with nurses. As did many parents, the Rogers sought out specialists and looked for a miracle cure. But they also realized that God's Plan may well involve Robin's early death. In a stunning passage, the child asked for God's forgiveness for a doctor who "said that babies who came into the world in my condition should be lined up in a row and 'machine-gunned,' because they were no good to themselves or to anybody else." After Robin's death, the Rogers family committed itself to advocating on behalf of all children with disabilities. In the book, referring to her parents, Robin says, "They're a lot stronger, since they got Our message."[35]

Rogers' book literally angelicized children with disabilities, offering a stark and potent contrast to views of disabled children as dark, bedeviled, cursed, or delinquent. Both Dale Rogers and Pearl Buck helped families of disabled children—especially parents—understand that they were not alone in their struggles, guilt, shame, or confusion.

In fact, well before either book was published, parents had sought ways to support each other in efforts to make their lives and those of their disabled children richer and more dignified. Informal groups formed in various states in the late 1930s and by the early 1950s had coalesced into formal associations. While professional associations of doctors, educators, and other professionals had formed in the 1800s around categories of disability—associations for the deaf, the blind, and the mentally disabled led the way—associations formed for parents and other advocates addressed purposes more social and political than scholarly or professional. The National Association of Parents and Friends of Retarded Children, the most high-profile of these, arose through the consolidated efforts of local advocacy groups and gained formal status in 1950. Between 1950 and 1980 the association changed its name and image several times, from the original name to the National Association for Retarded Children, the National Association for Retarded Citizens, and finally to its current name, The Arc. Eventually this organization would inspire other advocates for children with specific disabilities to form as well, bringing a much stronger voice to and for children with disabilities. By the 1960s and 1970s such groups, especially The Arc, had become major players in shaping and improving the lives of disabled children. The following chapter will examine how the National Association of Parents and Friends of Retarded Children, other organizations, the federal government, along with changing views of special education produced dramatic developments that affected the lives of children with disabilities between 1960 and 1980.[36]

NOTES

1. An excellent and concise example of such a call to reflection is Elise H. Martens, "Education for a Strong America," *Journal of Exceptional Children* 8 (November 1941): 36–41.

2. Goodwin Watson, "The Exceptional Child As a Neglected Resource," *Childhood Education* 14 (March 1938): 296–97.

3. Ibid., 297–99. *Educational Forum* 7 (January 1943): 157.

4. Andrew W. Hunt, "Child Accounting—Its Value From a Pedagogical and Administrative Standpoint," *Educational Forum* 7 (January 1943): 157.

5. Margaret A. Neuber, "Believe It—Or Not," *Journal of Exceptional Children* 7 (November 1940): 48–50.

6. Martens, "Education for a Strong America," 36, 39–41.

7. Edgar A. Doll, "The Exceptional Child in War Time," *Journal of Exceptional Children* 8 (April 1942): 204–5.

8. Watson B. Miller, "Education and the War," *Journal of Exceptional Children* 9 (May 1943): 237.

JOURNAL ARTICLES AND BOOK CHAPTERS

Addams, Jane. "The Home and the Special Child." *Addresses and Proceedings of the National Education Association* (1908): 1127–28.

Anderson, Hilma A. "The Smouse Opportunity School." *Journal of Exceptional Children* 4 (February 1938): 110–15.

Axline, Virginia M. "Understanding and Accepting the Child Who Is Blind." *Childhood Education* 30 (May 1954): 427–30.

Bacon, Albion Fellows. "The Mental Defective in the Home." *Indiana Bulletin* 107 (December 1916): 384–85.

Barbe, Walter B. "Locating Children with Emotional Problems." *Childhood Education* 30 (November 1953): 127–30.

Berry, Gordon. "Saving the Sight of School Children." *Journal of the National Education Association* 1 (1916): 816–19.

Biklen, Douglas. "Exclusion." *Peabody Journal of Education* 50 (April 1973): 226–34.

Blackmar, H. E., and Anna M. Kordsiemon. "Overcoming the Objection of Parents to the Special Class—Can It Be Done? How?" *Journal of the National Education Association* 3 (1918): 395–98.

Bliss, George. "President's Address: The Need of a Better Social Conscience." *Indiana Bulletin* 120 (March 1920): 26–28.

Bogdan, Robert. "'Does Mainstreaming Work?' Is a Silly Question." *Phi Delta Kappan* 64 (February 1983): 427–28.

Bryan, Mary. "As a Beginner Sees It." *Peabody Journal of Education* 16 (May 1939): 370–72.

Bryant, Keith N., and J. Cotter Hirschberg. "Helping the Parents of a Retarded Child: The Role of the Physician." *American Journal of Diseases of Children* 102 (July 1961): 82–96.

Budoff, Milton, and Jay Gottlieb. "Special-Class EMR Children Mainstreamed: A Study of an Aptitude (Learning Potential) X Treatment Interaction." *American Journal of Mental Deficiency* 81 (1976): 1–11.

Bullowa, Alma M. "The Need of Speech Work in the High Schools." *Journal of the National Education Association* 2 (1917): 865–68.

Butler, Amos W. "Some Families as Factors in Anti-Social Conditions." *Eugenics, Genetics and the Family* 1 (1923): 387–90.

Byers, James T. "Provision for the Feeble-Minded." *Proceedings and Papers of the Indiana State Teachers Association, 64th Annual Session* (1917): 168–71.

Carpenter, Doris E. "A Transportation Project for Retarded Boys." *Journal of Exceptional Children* 4 (December 1937): 56–60, 69.

Cegelka, Walter L., and James L. Tyler. "The Efficacy of Special Class Placement for the Mentally Retarded in Proper Perspective." *Training School Bulletin* 67 (1970): 33–68.

Cody, Frank. "How Detroit Provides for Its Atypical Children." *Journal of Education* 120 (June 7, 1937): 267–70.

Cohen, Marcella S. "The Visually Handicapped Child in the Rural Community." *Journal of Exceptional Children* 6 (April 1940): 260–63.

Cohen, Sol. "The Industrial Education Movement, 1906–1917." *American Quarterly* 20, no. 1 (1968): 95–110.

Comings, William R. "Are Mentality Tests on Right Lines?" *Educational Review* 64 (December 1922): 392–94.

———. "Crippled Children and Their Benefactors." *Journal of Education* 96 (December 28, 1922): 658–60.

"Crippled Children." *Journal of Education* 111 (January 27, 1930): 89.

Curtis, Henry S. "Salvaging the Crippled Child." *Journal of Education* 111 (April 14, 1930): 417.

Davison, Mabel. "Dramatizing Uncle Sam's Post Office." *Journal of Exceptional Children* 5 (January 1938): 89–92.

"Defectives." *Journal of Education* 93 (February 24, 1921): 212.

Dobbs, Harrison Allen. "Children with Defects: A Frame of Reference." *Peabody Journal of Education* 27 (January 1950): 228–36.

———. "Children with Defects: A Philosophical Proposal." *Peabody Journal of Education* 31 (September 1953): 67–77.

———. "Children with Defects: Steps Forward." *Peabody Journal of Education* 29 (November 1951): 157–65.

———. "More Certainty in Educating Children with Defects." *Peabody Journal of Education* 30 (September 1952): 66–74.

Doll, Edgar A. "The Exceptional Child in War Time." *Journal of Exceptional Children* 8 (April 1942): 204–6.

———. "School Training of Exceptional Children in Rural Districts." *The Training School Bulletin* 25 (June 1928): 49–58.

Draper, Anna Louise. "My Beginning Teaching Experiences." *Peabody Journal of Education* 16 (May 1939): 374–76.

Duggins, Lydia A. "Exceptional Children in the Classroom." *Journal of Education* 133 (October 1950): 200–2.

Dunn, Lloyd. "Special Education for the Mildly Retarded—Is Much of It Justifiable?" *Exceptional Children* 35 (September 1968): 5–22.

Edson, Andrew. "Education for the Handicapped." *Journal of Education* 94 (October 20, 1921): 383–84.

———. "Exceptional Children in Public Schools." *Journal of Education* 95 (June 1, 1922): 595–96.

Elliott, Bernice. "Learning to Teach Cripples." *Journal of Education* 115 (December 19, 1932): 691–93.

Estabrook, Arthur H. "Mental Defectiveness in Rural Communities." *Indiana Bulletin* 111 (June 1918): 244–48.

Farson, Mabel R. "Education of the Handicapped Child for Social Competency." *Journal of Exceptional Children* 6 (January 1940): 138–44, 150.

Feiner, Augusta L. "Dramatic Art in Detroit Special Education Classes." *Journal of Exceptional Children* 8 (May 1942): 255–257, 266–67.

Fernald, Walter E. "History of the Treatment of the Feebleminded." *Proceedings and Addresses of the National Education Association* (1893): 203–21.

Fitch, Waring James. "Detecting Handicapped Children in a Small Community." *Journal of Exceptional Children* 9 (April 1943): 210–11.

Foster, Josephine C., and Marion L. Mattson. "The Atypical Child in an Average School." *Childhood Education* 17 (November 1940): 120–24.

Franklin, Barry M. "Progressivism and Curriculum Differentiation: Special Classes in the Atlanta Public Schools, 1898–1923." *History of Education Quarterly* 29 (Winter 1989): 571–93.

Francis, George C. "Home Teaching for Crippled Children." *Journal of Education* III (June 16, 1930): 689.

Freeman, Frank N. "Sorting the Students." *Educational Review* 68 (November 1924): 169–74.

Gallaudet, Edward M. "Values in the Education of the Deaf." *Educational Review* 4 (June 1892): 16–26.

Gardner, Gladys. "The Nursery School Helps a Retarded Child." *Childhood Education* 21 (May 1945): 453–56.

Garrison, Ivan K. "A Broader Concept of Normalcy." *Journal of Education* 136 (March 1954): 178–81.

Gelb, Steven. "'Not Simply Bad and Incorrigible': Science, Morality, and Intellectual Deficiency." *History of Education Quarterly* 29 (Fall 1989): 359–79.

Gendel, Evalyn S. "Sex Education of the Mentally Retarded Child in the Home." Paper presented at the Council for Exceptional Children Convention, April 19, 1968. ARC Files, Drawer E.

Goodman, Hollace, Jay Gottlieb, and Robert H. Harrison. "Social Acceptance of EMRs Integrated into a Nongraded Elementary School." *American Journal of Mental Deficiency* 76 (1972): 412–17.

Gregory, Ida L. "The Child's New America." *Journal of Education* 102 (July 2, 1925): 11–12.

Groszmann, Maximilian P. E. "Special and Ungraded Classes." *Journal of Education* 95 (January 26, 1922): 102.

Guthrie, Elisabeth. "The Need for Knowing the Whole Child." *Journal of Exceptional Children* 4 (May 1938): 174–79, 183.

Hall, Inis B. "Practical Treatment of the Deaf-Blind." *Journal of Exceptional Children* 3 (April 1937): 102–6, 126.

Hansburg, Henry. "The Case of Daniel." *Childhood Education* 22 (September 1945): 37–40.

Hansen, Betty. "Day of Departure." Saginaw County *ARC Newsletter*, n.d., ARC Files, Drawer B.

———. "The Face of Truth." reprinted from the Saginaw County, Michigan *ARC Newsletter*, February 1960.

Hardwick, Rose S. "Types of Reading Disability." *Childhood Education* 8 (April 1932): 423–27.

Heffernan, Helen. "Meeting the Needs of Exceptional Children in Rural Schools." *Journal of Exceptional Children* 2 (October 1935): 49–50.

Hicks, Marjorie B. "Teaching Art to Backward Children." *Journal of Exceptional Children* 6 (February 1940): 172–75.

Hill, O. J. "Another Beam of Light through the Darkness." *Journal of Exceptional Children* 6 (January 1940): 129–37.

Hitch, Wanda. "School Teaching as Seen through the Eyes of a Beginning Teacher." *Peabody Journal of Education* 16 (May 1939): 378–81.

"How Children Differ—Working with Exceptions." *Childhood Education* 32 (January 1956): 208–20.

Hoyt, Franklin C. "The Juvenile Court of New York City." *Journal of the National Education Association* I (1916): 837–40.

Hunt, Andrew W. "Child Accounting—Its Value from a Pedagogical and Administrative Standpoint." *Educational Forum* 7 (January 1943): 157–60.

Ide, Gladys G. "Philadelphia's Orthopedic School." *Journal of Education* 120 (June 7, 1937): 274–76.

Indiana Bulletin 180 (March 1930): 62–81.

Inskeep, Annie Dolman. "Help for the Maladjusted Child." *Journal of Education* 120 (May 3, 1937): 217–21.

Jett, Carmel Leon. "My School in the Hills." *Peabody Journal of Education* 16 (May 1939): 383–86.

Johnson, Dallas D. "The Special Child and the Visiting Teacher." *Journal of the National Education Association* 2 (1917): 580–84.

Johnstone, E. R. "President's Address: The Function of the Special Class." *Addresses and Proceedings of the National Education Association* (1908): 1115–18.

———. "The Problem of the Feeble-Minded Child." *Indiana Bulletin* 107 (December 1916): 461–66.

Jones, Olive M. "Causes of Juvenile Delinquency." *Journal of Education* 96 (October 12, 1922): 350–52.

Knox, Margaret. "The Principal's Point of View of the Selection of Children for Special Classes." *Journal of the National Education Association* 2 (1917): 872–74.

Kordsiemon, Anna M. "Construction Work—Its Value in the Subnormal School." *Journal of the National Education Association* 2 (1917): 576–80.

Kugler, Edna M. "Efficient and Effective Classroom Management." *Journal of Exceptional Children* 2 (June 1936): 128–34, 138.

Kwiat, Charlotte. "Teaching in Little Hell." *Journal of Education* 133 (December 1950): 258–59.

Laird, Louise. "Teaching a Retarded Group." *Journal of Education* 121 (October 1938): 227–28.

Landau, Julia. "The Richmond Case Study: Ending Segregated Education for Disabled Children." In *Stepping Stones: Successful Advocacy for Children*, edited by Sheryl Dicker. New York: Foundation for Child Development, 1990.

Lavos, George. "Personality and a Physical Defect." *Journal of Exceptional Children* 7 (January 1941): 124–28, 145–146.

Laycock, Samuel R. "The Education of Exceptional Children in Smaller Cities or Rural Areas." *Journal of Exceptional Children* 2 (May 1935): 16–17.

———. "Problems in the Adolescence of Exceptional Children." *Journal of Exceptional Children* 9 (April 1943): 203–7.

Lazerson, Marvin. "The Origins of Special Education." In *Special Education Policies: Their History, Implementation, and Finance*, edited by Jay G. Chambers and William T. Hartman. Philadelphia: Temple University Press, 1983.

Leland, Bernice. "Case Study Approach to Difficulty in Reading." *Childhood Education* 13 (April 1937): 374–78.

Lenroot, Katharine F. "Delinquency Prevention through School and Social Agency Co-ordination." *Educational Forum* 8 (November 1943): 11–15.

Levy, Carrie B. "Milwaukee's Program of Special Education." *Journal of Exceptional Children* 8 (February 1942): 132–143.

Lilly, M. Stephen. "A Teapot in a Tempest." *Exceptional Children* 37 (September 1970): 43–49.

Lord, Arthur B. "The Mentally Retarded." *Journal of Education* 107 (May 28, 1928): 635–36.

Louttit, C. M., and Gladys D. Frith. "The Dorbets—A Feebleminded Family." *The Journal of Abnormal and Social Psychology* 29 (October–December 1934): 301–13.

Lovelace, Sarah. "Our Classroom." *Peabody Journal of Education* 16 (May 1939): 372–74.

Luckey, Bertha M., A. H. Sutherland, and Frank Cody. "The Practical Value of Psychological Tests—Do They Find the Bright and Dull Pupils?" *Journal of the National Education Association* 3 (1918): 388–94.

Lynch, Katherine D. "Enrichment of the Program for Subnormal Children." *Journal of Exceptional Children* 5 (November 1938): 49–53.

Lyon, Miss. "Speech Improvement in the Chicago Public Schools." *Journal of the National Education Association* 2 (1917): 864–65.

Marquis, Irene. "Helping the Visually Handicapped." *Journal of Education* 134 (March–April 1951): 106–7.

Martens, Elise H. "Education for a Strong America." *Journal of Exceptional Children* 8 (November 1941): 36–41.

Martin, Frederick. "The Problem of the Speech Defective." *Journal of Education* 106 (August 29, 1927): 162–63.

McClancy, Joseph V. S. "Preserving the Family." *Journal of the National Education Association* 1 (1916): 848–50.

McHugh, Caroline L. "Boston Has Hospital School." *Journal of Education* 111 (June 16, 1930): 688–89.

Mendenhall, Georgiana S. "The Influence of the Arts on the Lives of Handicapped Children." *Journal of Exceptional Children* 7 (October 1940): 11–18, 33–34.

Miller, Watson B. "Education and the War." *Journal of Exceptional Children* 9 (May 1943): 237.

Mitchell, Vethake E. "Oral Deformities in Their Relation to Defective Speech." *Journal of the National Education Association* 2 (1917): 869.

Moise, Lotte E. "Will the Real Advocate for Retarded Persons Please Stand Up!" Reprinted from *Child Welfare*, January 1975. ARC Files, Drawer E.

Moore, Joseph A. "Luring the Laggard." *Journal of Education* 121 (May 1938): 166.

Mortenson, Peter A. "Crippled Children." *Journal of Education* 97 (March 29, 1923): 342.

Murray, Mrs. Max A. "Needs of Parents of Mentally Retarded Children." New York: National Association of Retarded Children, 1969. ARC Files, Drawer D.

Myers, James K. "The Efficacy of the Special Day School for EMR Pupils." *Mental Retardation* 14 (August 1976): 3–11.

National Association for Retarded Children. "How to Aid the Retarded." 1962: 1–5. ARC Files, Drawer C.

National Association for Retarded Children, Public Institutions Committee. "Creating Better Relationship Between Parents and Institutions." Paper presented at the Public Institutions Workshop, NARC Convention, 1958. ARC Files, Drawer B.

Nesbitt, Marion. " . . . When the 'Different' Child Is Accepted." *Childhood Education* 27 (January 1951): 218–19.

Neuber, Margaret A. "Believe It—Or Not." *Journal of Exceptional Children* 7 (November 1940): 48–53, 78.

Nutterville, Catherine. "Equality of Educational Opportunity for the Slow-Learning Pupils in High School." *Journal of Exceptional Children* 7 (January 1941): 133–37.

Osgood, Robert L. "The Menace of the Feebleminded: George Bliss, Amos Butler, and the Indiana Committee on Mental Defectives." *Indiana Magazine of History* 97 (December 2001): 253–77.

———. "Undermining the Common School Ideal: Intermediate Schools and Ungraded Classes in Boston, 1838–1900." *History of Education Quarterly* 37 (Winter 1997): 375–98.

Palen, Imogen B. "The Hard of Hearing Child in the Public Schools." *Journal of Education* 103 (January 7, 1926): 11–12.

Patry, Frederick L. "Teaching the Handicapped Child." *Journal of Education* 116 (September 4, 1933): 333–35.

Perske, Robert A. "An Attempt to Find and Adequate Theological View of Mental Retardation." Paper presented at the conference on "The Church and the Mentally Retarded," Nebraska Psychiatric Institute, April 1965, ARC Files, Drawer A;

Peter, Lily. "An Adventure in Educational Democracy." *Peabody Journal of Education* 17 (September 1939): 111–14.

Plimpton, Harriet. "My Experiment with the Misfit High School Girls." *Educational Review* 68 (November 1924): 178–180.

Radcliffe, Margaret Williams. "The Hard of Hearing Child in Our Schools." *Childhood Education* 21 (May 1945): 457–59, 478.

Reed, Anna Y. "How Deal with Our Youthful Morons?" *Journal of Education* 107 (March 26, 1928): 383–85.

Reed, Frank A. "Speech Work in the Detroit Public Schools." *Journal of the National Education Association* 2 (1917): 865.

Reigart, John F. "Speech-Correction as a School Problem." *Journal of the National Education Association* 2 (1917): 868–69.

Rich, Frank M. "Paterson Educates the Handicapped." *Journal of Education* 112 (October 6, 1930): 232–33.

Riggs, James G. "Training of Teachers for Special Classes." *Journal of the National Education Association* 2 (1917): 879–81.

Scarborough, Willie H. "A Letter to Parents." 1954, ARC Files, Drawer C.

Schreiber, Meyer, and Mary Feeley. "Siblings of the Retarded." reprinted from *Children* (November–December 1965). ARC Files, Drawer E.

Sheldon, Marjorie P. "Protection of the Crippled Child from Avoidable Strain in School." *Journal of Exceptional Children* 8 (November 1940): 50–56.

Shimer, Edgar Dubs. "The Delinquent." *Journal of the National Education Association* 1 (1916): 840–841.

Snedden, David. "The Public School and Juvenile Delinquency." *Educational Review* 33 (April 1907): 374–85.

Strachan, Louise. "New Ways for Old in the Care of Delicate Children," *Journal of Exceptional Children* 1 (December 1935): 60–65.

Stein, Vita. "Living Democracy—A Classroom Experience of Children with Multiple Handicaps." *Journal of Exceptional Children* 8 (January 1942): 107–8, 122.

Stewart, Alma May. "Personnel Work with the Special School Pupil." *Journal of Exceptional Children* 6 (May 1940): 283–87, 306–7.

Strait, Suzanne Hart. "Bringing Up a Retarded Child." reprinted from *Parents' and Better Homemaking Magazine* 37 (December 1962). ARC Files, Drawer A.

Stullken, Edward H. "Special Education in Chicago." *Journal of Exceptional Children* 1 (December 1935): 73–75.

Sutherland, Ida M. "Divergent Views." *Exceptional Children* 4 (October 1937): 20–21.

———. "How Los Angeles Takes Care of Her Exceptional Children." *Journal of Exceptional Children* 4 (April 1938): 159–65.

"They Discovered a New Dimension of Love." reprinted from *Today's Health*, February 1959. ARC Files, Drawer D.

Thompson, Vesta S. "Poetry and the Exceptional Child." *Journal of Exceptional Children* 3 (December 1936): 34–38.

Thurston, Henry W. "The Social Worker." *Journal of the National Education Association* 1 (1916): 850–51.

Tillinghast, E. S. "The Oral Method of Education of the Deaf." *Journal of the National Education Association* 2 (1917): 572–76.

Tropea, Joseph L. "Bureaucratic Order and Special Children: Urban Schools, 1890s–1940s." *History of Education Quarterly* 27 (Spring 1987): 29–53.

———. "Bureaucratic Order and Special Children: Urban Schools, 1950s–1960s." *History of Education Quarterly* 27 (Fall 1987): 341–61.

Valentine, P. F. "They Blame the Home for Delinquency." *Educational Forum* 11 (March 1947): 285–87.

Vernon, McCay. "Education's 'Three Mile Island': PL 94-142." *Peabody Journal of Education* 59 (1981–1982): 24–29.

Warner, M. LaVinia. "Problems of the Delinquent Girl." *Journal of Exceptional Children* 7 (December 1940): 102–7, 112.

Waskowitz, Charlotte H. "The Parents of Retarded Children Speak for Themselves." Reprinted by NARC from the *Journal of Pediatrics* (March 1959): 1–16. ARC Files, Drawer D.

Watson, Goodwin. "The Exceptional Child as a Neglected Resource." *Childhood Education* 14 (March 1938): 296–99.

Watson, P. M. "Cleveland's School for Problem Boys." *Journal of Education* 112 (December 15, 1930): 499–500.

Wood, Thomas D. "Discussion." *Addresses and Proceedings of the National Education Association* (1903): 1003–4.

Young, Herman H. "Experiments in Public Schools." *Indiana Bulletin* 136 (March 1924): 26.

Zufelt, Olga S. "Sheboygan Makes Handicapped Happy." *Journal of Education* 112 (October 27, 1930): 315–16.

PUBLIC DOCUMENTS

Boston School Committee. *20th Annual Report of the Superintendent of the Boston Public Schools.* Boston, MA, 1900.

Illinois Commission for Handicapped Children. *The Handicapped Child in the Mainstream: Proceedings of the Tenth Governor's Conference on Exceptional Children.* Chicago: Commission for Handicapped Children, 1953.

Indiana School for Feebleminded Youth. *Annual Reports of the Indiana School for Feebleminded Youth.* Indianapolis, IN: 1892, 1893, 1894, 1898.

Indiana State Archives, Commission on Public Records, Fort Wayne School for Feebleminded Youth, Inmate Packets 1-29, Box R1887–030671.

Massachusetts Advocacy Center, *Out of the Mainstream: Education of Disabled Youth in Massachusetts.* Boston, MA: Massachusetts Advocacy Center, 1987.

National Council on Disability. *Achieving Independence: The Challenge for the 21st Century: A Decade of Progress in Disability Policy; Setting an Agenda for the Future.* Washington, DC: GPO, 1996.

Otey, Elizabeth Lewis. *Report on Condition of Woman and Child Wage-Earners in the United States. Volume VI: The Beginnings of Child Labor Legislation in Certain States; a Comparative Study.* Washington, DC: Government Printing Office, 1910.

President's Committee on Mental Retardation. *Hello World.* GPO 1968-0-308-222. Washington, DC: GPO, 1986.

———. *MR 76: Mental Retardation: Past and Present.* Washington, DC: GPO, 1977.

———. *Report to the President: The National Reform Agenda and Citizens with Mental Retardation; A Journey of Renewal for All Americans.* Washington, DC: GPO, 1994.

Sloan, William and Harvey A. Stevens. *A Century of Decision: A History of the American Association on Mental Deficiency 1876–1976.* Washington, DC: GPO, 1976.

Special Class Teachers Club of Boston. *The Boston Way: Plans for the Development of the Individual Child.* 4th ed. Boston, MA, 1928.

State of Indiana. *General Laws, 1879,* Chapter VIII, Sec. 2.

———. "Report of Decatur County Superintendent," *Report of the Superintendent of Public Instruction.* Indianapolis, IN, 1872/1873, 1881/1882.

———. *34th Report of the Superintendent of Public Instruction Being the 13th Biennial Report.* Indianapolis, IN, 1885/1886.

———. *36th Report of the Superintendent of Public Instruction, Being the 14th Biennial Report.* Indianapolis, IN, 1897/1898.

———. *24th Biennial Report of the State Superintendent of Public Instruction.* Indianapolis, IN, 1907/1908: 109.

Wallace, Anna M. "History of the Walter E. Fernald State School." n.d.: unpublished manuscript in author's possession.

White House Conference on Child Health and Protection. *The Handicapped Child: Report of the Committee on Physically and Mentally Handicapped.* New York: Century, 1933.

Wightman, Joseph M., comp. *Annals of the Boston Primary School Committee, from Its First Establishment in 1818, to Its Dissolution in 1855.* Boston, MA: Rand and Avery, 1860.

Name Index

Subject Index

About the Author

ROBERT L. OSGOOD is Associate Professor of Education, Indiana University, Purdue University, Indianapolis.